ESSENTIAL SKILLS FOR EFFECTIVE SCHOOL LEADERSHIP

Frank Siccone

PEARSON

Boston Columbus Indianapolis New York San Francisco Upper Saddle River
Amsterdam Cape Town Dubai London Madrid Milan Munich Paris Montreal Toronto
Delhi Mexico City São Paulo Sydney Hong Kong Seoul Singapore Taipei Tokyo

Vice President and Editorial Director: Jeffery W. Johnston
Senior Acquisitions Editor: Meredith D. Fossel
Associate Editor: Anne Whittaker
Editorial Assistant: Nancy Holstein
Vice President, Director of Marketing: Margaret Waples
Senior Marketing Manager: Christopher Barry
Senior Managing Editor: Pamela D. Bennett
Project Manager: Kerry Rubadue
Production Manager: Laura Messerly
Senior Art Director: Jayne Conte
Cover Designer: Suzanne Duda
Cover Art: Fotolia
Full-Service Project Management/Composition: TexTech International Pvt.Ltd.
Printer/Binder: R.R. Donnelley & Sons
Cover Printer: R.R. Donnelley & Sons
Text Font: Minion

Credits and acknowledgments for material borrowed from other sources and reproduced, with permission, in this textbook appear on the appropriate pages within the text.

Every effort has been made to provide accurate and current Internet information in this book. However, the Internet and information posted on it are constantly changing, so it is inevitable that some of the Internet addresses listed in this textbook will change.

Library of Congress Cataloging-in-Publication Data

Siccone, Frank, 1948–
   Essential skills for effective school leadership / Frank Siccone.
      p. cm.
   Includes bibliographical references and index.
   ISBN-13: 978-0-13-138519-1
   ISBN-10: 0-13-138519-4
      1. Educational leadership—United States.   2. School administrators—United States.
3. School management and organization.   I. Title.
   LB2805.S5855 2012
   371.2'011—dc23

2011023374

10 9 8 7 6 5 4 3 2 1

ISBN 10: 0-13-138519-4
ISBN 13: 978-0-13-138519-1

CONTENTS

PREFACE

*If your actions inspire others to dream more, learn more, do more
and become more, you are a leader.*

—JOHN QUINCY ADAMS

WHY SCHOOL LEADERSHIP MATTERS

Effective schools require effective leadership.

Among all school-related factors that contribute to what students learn at school, leadership is second only to classroom instruction. In fact, the effects of leadership on student learning account for about a quarter of total school results. Furthermore, the same review of the research shows that effective leadership has an even more profound influence in turning around underperforming schools.

School reform efforts simply cannot succeed unless successful leaders remain at the school for an extended period of time. Research on organizational change suggests that leaders need at least five years for successful implementation of large-scale change. Yet recent data on principal retention reveal that 52% of principals had left within a three-year period. Turnover rates are higher for middle and high school principals, and higher still in schools in which more than 50% of the students are economically disadvantaged. Research also indicates that high principal turnover leads to higher teacher turnover, which, in turn, has a negative impact on student achievement.[1]

Clearly, more needs to be done to support educational leaders in meeting the many challenges of running today's schools.

SCHOOL LEADERSHIP DEVELOPMENT:
THE BASICS AND BEYOND

There is no ideal school leader profile and no single leadership style that works best in all situations. Effective leaders need an expansive repertoire of practices and the wisdom and flexibility to be able to adapt to various leadership roles and to the unique demands of the particular set of circumstances. This book attempts to provide you with not only some of the basic skills of effective leaders but also the tools for being able to respond in productive ways to meet the dynamic and challenging needs specific to your school community.

There will be times when you need to be passionate and persuasive in order to activate and motivate the community on behalf of what's best for students. In other situations, it will be your ability to be decisive in driving for results that will sustain people's commitment and confidence in your leadership. Frequently, you will be called on to facilitate a spirit of collaboration so that all the members of the community are inspired to work together to improve teaching and learning. Being responsible for retaining the big picture focus on a shared vision while holding others accountable for implementing detailed action plans are two dimensions of the leadership challenge that you need to balance. Whether the situation calls for change that is incremental or transformational, the lessons in this book will contribute to your ability to succeed.

ESSENTIAL SKILLS FOR EFFECTIVE SCHOOL LEADERSHIP

Leaders in general, and school leaders in particular, share five essential sets of skills:

1. *Confidence.* Leaders believe in themselves and in their ability to mobilize others to act. They inspire confidence in others by being clear about their vision, by being competent in delivering on what they promise, and by caring about the concerns of others.
2. *Communication.* Leaders are effective communicators. They are able to articulate what they mean with the clarity needed to transform words into deeds and rhetoric into results. Leaders listen. They are skilled in shaping the context of conversations so that shared meaning is created and common understandings lead to productive outcomes.
3. *Collaboration.* Leaders recognize that success is a team effort. They know that people support what they help create. By engaging others in setting goals, planning strategies, and solving problems together, leaders expand their capacity to effect change throughout the organization.
4. *Coaching.* Leaders invest time and energy into developing their team. They assess their own strengths and weaknesses as well as those of the rest of the team, and create an environment where ongoing professional growth is encouraged and supported.
5. *Continuous Improvement.* Leaders view change as an opportunity. If the status quo is adequate, then you need an administrator not a leader. Knowing that change unmanaged can lead to chaos, successful leaders are proactive in terms of anticipating how to keep improvement efforts on track.

The purpose of this book is to help you develop these five skills. The material in the book is aligned with Educational Leadership Policy Standards: ISLLC 2008, which represent the broad, high-priority themes that education leaders must address in order to promote the success of every student.[2] The six standards are listed here along with the parts of the book that most directly correlate to each.

Standard 1: An education leader promotes the success of every student by facilitating the development, articulation, implementation, and stewardship of a vision of learning that is shared and supported by all stakeholders.

Part Five: To Lead Is to Succeed—Continuous Improvement Skills This section of the book provides lessons related to collaboratively developing and implementing a shared vision and mission, collecting and using data to identify goals, assessing organizational effectiveness and promoting organizational learning, creating and implementing plans to achieve goals, promoting continuous and sustainable improvement, and monitoring and evaluating progress and revising plans as needed.

Standard 2: An education leader promotes the success of every student by advocating, nurturing, and sustaining a school culture and instructional program conducive to student learning and staff professional growth.

Part Three: To Lead Is to Align—Collaboration Skills This entire section of the book relates to nurturing and sustaining a culture of collaboration, trust, learning, and high expectations.

Part Four: To Lead Is to Teach—Coaching Skills Lessons in this section relate to creating a personalized and motivating learning environment for students, supervising instruction, and developing the instructional and leadership capacity of staff.

Standard 3: An education leader promotes the success of every student by ensuring management of the organization, operation, and resources for a safe, efficient, and effective learning environment.

Part Three: To Lead Is to Align—Collaboration Skills The decision-making model in this section is an excellent tool related to developing the capacity for distributed leadership.

Part Five: To Lead Is to Succeed—Continuous Improvement Skills This section also relates to developing the capacity for distributed leadership, as well as to obtaining, allocating, aligning, and efficiently utilizing human, fiscal, and technological resources, and to ensuring teacher and organizational time is focused to support quality instruction and student learning.

Standard 4: An education leader promotes the success of every student by collaborating with faculty and community members, responding to diverse community interests and needs, and mobilizing community resources.

Part Two: To Lead Is to Listen—Communication Skills and Part Three: To Lead Is to Align—Collaboration Skills Both these sections relate to promoting understanding, appreciation, and use of the community's diverse cultural, social, and intellectual resources and to building and sustaining positive, productive relationships.

> **Standard 5:** *An education leader promotes the success of every student by acting with integrity, fairness, and in an ethical manner.*

Part One: To Lead Is to Learn—Confidence Skills This section relates to modeling principles of self-awareness, reflective practice, transparency, and ethical behavior; safeguarding the values of democracy, equity, and diversity; considering and evaluating the potential moral and legal consequences of decision making; promoting social justice; and ensuring that individual student needs inform all aspects of schooling.

> **Standard 6:** *An education leader promotes the success of every student by understanding, responding to, and influencing the political, social, economic, legal, and cultural context.*

Part Two: To Lead Is to Listen—Communication Skills This section on communication stresses the critical importance of context.

AS YOU DEVELOP YOUR LEADERSHIP SKILLS

If you are an individual school leader—or an aspiring one—you will discover the leadership lessons contained in this book to be easy-to-understand and ready-to-use. In order to make this a valuable resource for every reader, it is designed so that you can pick and choose the topics that are most relevant to your situation and customize your own individual leadership development program.

Many of the exercises are intended to be used in a collaborative team environment, which might include a district-sponsored leadership cohort or book study group or an on-site school improvement team or instructional leadership team. The material would also work extremely well as a comprehensive collection of workshop handouts for a leadership course; at summer academies for prospective principals, assistant principals, and teacher leaders; and in other professional development trainings.

In 1970, the year I started my graduate studies in education, Charles E. Silberman's book, *Crisis in the Classroom* was published. If someone had told me that 40 years after this sobering wake-up call, we would still be dealing with a crisis in our schools, I would not have believed it. When I think about some of the amazing accomplishments that have been achieved in other fields, I'm saddened to realize that comparable breakthroughs have not occurred in education. The problems in today's schools deserve everyone's attention and involvement. I'm writing this book because I want to be part of the solution.

Frank Siccone
May 2011
San Francisco, California

ABOUT THE AUTHOR

 *Frank Siccone, Ed.D.,* is an educator, author, and organizational leadership consultant. For three decades, he has offered workshops to teachers and administrators throughout the country and conducted youth leadership training for students not only in the United States, but also from Russia and South Africa.

Dr. Siccone has written another book on school leadership titled, *The Power to Lead: A Guide for School Administrators on Facilitating Change.* His first book, *101 Ways to Develop Student Self-Esteem and Responsibility*, was co-authored with Jack Canfield (co-author of *Chicken Soup for the Soul*). Dr. Siccone's books have been translated into Chinese, Czech, Russian, and Spanish. He has taught classes and workshops at several colleges and universities including the California State University, East Bay and San Bernardino; San Francisco State University; University of California, Riverside; the University of San Francisco; and the Leadership Institute at Yale University.

In addition to his work in education, Frank has also consulted with an impressive list of corporate clients such as Cisco Systems, Hitachi, Intel, Pepsi Cola, Sprint, Sun Microsystems, and Walmart.com. Among the nonprofit organizations with whom he has worked recently are the California Association of Student Councils, the American Society of Plastic Surgeons, and Green For All.

ACKNOWLEDGMENTS

There are so many people who should be acknowledged for contributing in innumerable ways to my personal and professional growth. The insights, strategies, and tools reflected in this book were inspired by great teachers and by insightful students wise beyond their years.

Let me start by thanking the wonderful team at Pearson Education for their support in getting this project completed successfully—Steve Dragin, Meredith Fossel, Anne Whittaker, Kerry Rubadue, Nancy Holstein, Patti Brecht, and Vijayakumar S. I'm grateful also to the group of reviewers whose feedback added significantly to the quality of the final product: Joyce Edwards, Duxbury Public Schools; John Gabriel, Park View High School; Pamela Van Horn, Kilbourne Middle School; Rebecca McBride, University of West Florida; Peter Osroff, Garden City Middle School; and Marilyn Underwood, Marion County Public Schools.

Another important contributor was Dee Baker, Superintendent at Washington Union School District in Monterey County, California. She and her team offered suggestions for how to make this book a valuable resource for today's school leaders. Dee is one of a long list of educators whom I count among my personal friends. They include among others: JoAnn Bailey, Kreg Baker, Rob Beaumont, Jack Canfield, Ricky Capsuto, Patricia and Roger Madsen, Meladee and Hanoch McCarty, Linda Pearson, Jan Phillips Paulsen, Pat Robak, Joyce and Leon Spreyer, Ricardo Tellez, John Tweten, and Esther Wright.

During the development of these lessons in leadership, I've had the good fortune to work with a wide range of clients—small and large businesses and nonprofit organizations as well as schools. I am grateful to all of them for providing me with real-world opportunities to test and refine the material contained in this book. In this context, I especially want to acknowledge June Thompson and the truly outstanding student leaders at the California Association of Student Councils (CASC). Also, let me recognize the leadership team and staff at Green For All, where I was literally moved to tears by the bravery of their mission of eliminating poverty while saving the planet. As for corporate clients, they don't get any better than Sara Ortloff Khoury and her colleagues at Walmart.com. Thanks also to Dan Bellack, Steve Darland, and Kim and Ray McKewon for providing opportunities for me to expand my capacity to contribute in new directions.

Laura Aragon at Interaction Associates, Paul Ferrari at CCSSO, Jim Garrison at Community Boards, and Charlotte Roberts at Blue Fire Partners were instrumental in securing the permissions needed to adapt material for the book, and Alex Linder helped with the proofreading.

I would like to dedicate this book to the memory of two very special people—both of them were talented educators and extraordinary human beings. Holly Horton, the Head of School at Live Oak School in San Francisco, had incredible strength grounded in deep compassion. Robert Wright worked with me for many years until he was diagnosed with leukemia. At that point, he realized it was time to pursue his dream of living in Asia and being a full-time teacher, for it was there that life was most meaningful and he felt most fulfilled. He spent his last few years teaching at the University in Bangkok.

Finally, thanks to my family and to Chris Jehle, my partner in life, for helping me fulfill my purpose for being in a relationship—to love and be loved unconditionally.

PART ONE

TO LEAD IS TO LEARN— CONFIDENCE SKILLS
7 Ways to Build Confidence in Your Leadership

A university professor went to visit Nan-in, a famous Japanese master to inquire about Zen. While the master quietly served tea, the professor talked incessantly about Zen as if he knew everything there was to know about the topic. The master poured the visitor's cup to the brim, and then kept pouring. The professor watched the overflowing cup until he could no longer restrain himself. "It's already full!" he exclaimed. "No more will go in!" "Like this cup, you are already full," Nan-in replied.

Unless the professor were willing to let go of his preexisting beliefs and opinions, there wouldn't be any room for him to experience new and more profound insights. Or as the Zen master put it, "How can I show you Zen unless you first empty your cup?"

—TRADITIONAL ZEN STORY

You are invited to approach the material in this book with a learner's mindset. This book is about learning to lead. It is also about leading to learn.

Much has been written in the past two decades about the concept of transforming schools into Professional Learning Communities, and research supports the assumption that student learning increases when educators participate in learning communities. There is considerable evidence that suggests that when the school principal is actively involved in continuous learning, this contributes greatly to creating a culture that facilitates the professional development of teachers, which—if focused on instructional practices—results in consistent improvement for students. According to a report by the National Staff Development Council, "Strengthening the skills and knowledge of the nation's 100,000 principals is likely to have more immediate payoff in raising student performance than any other area of school improvement because it is central to raising standards, improving teacher quality, and holding schools accountable for results."[1]

This first section puts you in the role of "learner-in-chief" so that you are demonstrating by example that the learning process can be as challenging as it is exhilarating. By increasing your knowledge, setting professional development goals, practicing new skills, expanding beyond your comfort zone, and gaining greater confidence in your capacity to be an effective leader, you have the power to inspire the rest of the school community to learn to love learning.

You will start your journey, as all good learners should, with a self-assessment that will enable you to reflect on which areas of leadership you should target as growth opportunities. The next two sets of activities help you define your core beliefs and values so that you are able to speak with greater clarity about where you want to lead your school community. Not only is it important that you have confidence in yourself, but it is equally as important that others have confidence in you. Therefore, a series of activities is included to help you understand how to build trust by being effective, ethical, and responsible. You will be asked to dream big, and to act boldly.

1. Leading To Learn

*We are not what we know but what
we are willing to learn.*

—Mary Catherine Bateson

PURPOSE

Part One of this book is entitled *To Lead Is To Learn*. It is an invitation for you to embrace the mindset of a learner embarking on a process of discovering new insights, acquiring new tools, and enhancing your leadership skills. The purpose of this activity is to encourage you to set learning goals for yourself so that you can gain maximum benefit from reading this book and practicing the Leadership Learning Experiences contained in each section.

A good place to start is with a baseline assessment of your current strengths as a leader as well as of opportunities for future growth.

Effective School Leaders Self-Assessment Worksheet

To what extent do you engage in the following behaviors? Choose the number that best applies to each statement and record it in the blank to the left of the statement.

1 = Almost never, 2 = Seldom, 3 = About half the time, 4 = Usually, 5 = Almost always

_____ I consider myself a life-long learner and actively seek out opportunities to develop new skills and expand my knowledge.

_____ I am honest with myself about my strengths as well as my limitations.

_____ I am effective in setting realistic goals for myself, and then following through to achieve them.

_____ I have a clear philosophy about education, and I am able to communicate this to the school community.

_____ I am able to communicate the importance of education in a way that inspires and motivates students, staff, and the community.

_____ I am consistent in acting with integrity, with fairness, and in an ethical manner.

(*continues*)

Effective School Leaders Self-Assessment Worksheet, *continued*

_____ I model responsible behavior by taking ownership for my actions and their consequences.

_____ I am confident in my ability to demonstrate the attitudes and skills necessary to succeed.

_____ I am open and honest about how I like to work, and how I make decisions, so that people trust that I am doing what I think is best for the school—whether they necessarily agree with me or not.

_____ I do my best to maintain a sense of humor in order to keep things in perspective and avoid taking things too seriously.

_____ I listen to diverse points of view.

_____ I am effective in asking probing questions to ensure that I understand the meaning of someone's communication.

_____ I have the skills to engage in productive conversations with people whose communication styles are different from mine.

_____ I have a clear set of guidelines for when and how to involve stakeholders in the decision-making process.

_____ I am able to build consensus among diverse members of the community.

_____ I know how to engage people in solving problems in a collaborative manner.

_____ I challenge people to take appropriate action to solve problems, not just complain about them.

_____ I have the wisdom to know which problems are in our control to solve and which ones are not.

_____ I have the negotiation skills that enable me to help others resolve conflicts successfully.

_____ I recognize that in my job some situations do not lend themselves to simple solutions, and I know how to manage these dilemmas fairly well.

_____ I consistently take the time to express my appreciation for people's contributions, and to acknowledge their accomplishments.

_____ I know how to give constructive feedback that is directive and supportive.

_____ I make it safe for people to give me feedback so that I can continue to improve my effectiveness.

_____ I use my influence as a leader to inspire people's commitment to our goals rather than to try to force them into compliance.

_____ I am an educator who recognizes and supports different learning styles among adults as well as students.

_____ I am comfortable sharing leadership responsibility with staff.

_____ I am fully engaged in facilitating the development, articulation, implementation, and stewardship of a vision of learning that is shared and supported by the school community.

_____ I am experienced in the principles and processes of developing and implementing strategic plans.

_____ I challenge myself and the staff to constantly search for new and innovative ways to improve how we promote the success of all students.

_____ I can be counted on to keep us focused on what matters most—student success.

PROCEDURE

1. Locate the *Effective School Leaders Self-Assessment Worksheet* containing 30 leadership behaviors for you to rate. In selecting each response, be realistic about the extent to which you actually engage in the behavior. Do not answer in terms of how you would like to see yourself or in terms of what you should be doing. Answer in terms of how you typically behave—on most days, on most projects, and with most people. If your leadership role is in the classroom and school, think about how you behave with your colleagues and students. If you work in reform initiatives at the district, regional, or state levels, think about how you behave in this role.

2. Based on the self-assessment you just completed, reflect on the items that you scored the highest, and acknowledge these as strengths that you have which you should continue to practice.

3. Next, reflect on the items that you scored the lowest, and recognize that these are learning opportunities for you.

4. Choose three items from the *Effective School Leaders Self-Assessment Worksheet* that you would like to focus on as you read this book, paying particular attention to the sections that relate to the leadership skills you are most interested in improving. Restate these three assessment items as learning outcomes on the *Leadership Learning Outcomes Worksheet.*

For example, assessment item 13 on the Effective School Leaders Self-Assessment Worksheet: *I have the skills to engage in productive conversations with people whose communication styles are different from mine* might be reworded as a goal in the following way: *The outcome I intend to achieve by reading this book is to become a more effective communicator by increasing my understanding of communication styles and by practicing ways of modifying my approach to working with different people.*

Leadership Learning Outcomes Worksheet

Use your completed Effective School Leaders Self-Assessment Worksheet to create three learning outcomes:

OUTCOME 1

OUTCOME 2

OUTCOME 3

2. Leading With Vision

*If I ran a school, I'd give the average grade to the ones
who gave me all the right answers, for being good
parrots. I'd give the top grades to those who made a lot
of mistakes and told me about them, and then told me
what they learned from them.*

—R. BUCKMINSTER FULLER

PURPOSE

To be a truly effective leader, you must know where you are going, and to know where you are going, you must know where you are coming from. Beliefs influence actions.

The purpose of this activity is for you to create greater clarity about your beliefs regarding education and to organize your beliefs into a coherent and compelling vision. Articulating your vision will enable you to focus with greater precision, communicate with greater conviction, and lead with greater confidence.

A Vision Statement describes where you are going, the direction you are taking, and the destination you imagine. An effective vision projects a compelling story about the future. It appeals to the long-term interests of major stakeholders. The vision reflects ambitious yet achievable goals. It is both focused yet flexible, clear, and easy to communicate.

Compare these Vision Statements from a number of different schools, individual school leaders, and other types of organizations:

- To be recognized as leaders in child and family development by providing the highest-quality, comprehensive, seamless services based on community assessment. (Monterey County Head Start)
- Benjamin Banneker Elementary School is dedicated to producing literate, competent, responsible students who will be able to reason critically, and become functioning and productive members of the school, community, and the broader society. School personnel will have high expectations for students, including those with special needs. A learning environment will be created that is conducive for students to achieve higher levels of academic performance, so that they may reach their goals in life. (Chicago, 2006)

- Cherokee Middle School shall be a community nurturing academic excellence for all students and demonstrating leadership in character development. (Springfield, MO, 2009)
- Troy High School will become an exemplary learning community that supports innovation and is committed to continuous improvement. THS will address the academic, social, emotional, and physical needs of its learners. Troy High School will be a place where a collaborative community develops curriculum, instructional strategies, and assessment to ensure all students learn. (Troy, MI, 2009)
- All students will graduate. As a result, they are caring, competent, and critical thinkers, fully informed, engaged, and contributing citizens, and prepared to succeed in college and career. (Oakland Unified School District, Oakland, CA, 2010)
- Become the Harvard of the West. (Stanford University, 1940s)
- Democratize the automobile. (Ford Motor Company, early 1900s)
- Put a man on the moon by the end of the decade. (NASA, 1960)

PROCEDURE

1. Imagine that you were just informed that you have been selected to receive the National Distinguished School Leader Award. You have been asked to submit a one-to-three sentence statement describing your vision for schools, which will be published in this organization's newsletter and on its Web site.
2. In preparation for writing your vision, answer the questions on the *Vision Statement Worksheet.*
3. Share the draft of your Vision Statement with a colleague to solicit feedback. Suggest that he or she use the following structure for offering positive comments as well as helpful suggestions.

   - In general, what do you like about the Vision Statement?
   - More specifically, how well does the Vision Statement achieve the following objectives? For each objective, give examples from the Vision Statement where this was done well, and offer suggestions about how this might be done even more effectively.

     - The Vision Statement paints a clear before-and-after picture of what's true about the school now, and what will be true after the school leader's vision is realized.
     - The Vision Statement contains specific, concrete examples to explain and illustrate the school leader's goal for the school and strategy for achieving it.
     - The Vision Statement reveals evidence of a personal commitment to leading the school in a positive direction expressed in an authentic manner.
     - This Vision Statement gives you confidence in the school leader's ability to deliver on this commitment.

4. Consider rewriting the Vision Statement based on the feedback you received, and decide if you might like to disseminate it to members of your school community.

Vision Statement Worksheet

1. What concerns you most about the current situation at your school, or about education in general?

2. What is your vision of where you would like to see your school be in three to five years?

3. What is your strategy for leading the school from where it is to where you envision it being?

4. What research data support your view that this strategy can lead to the outcomes you envision?

5. What leadership skills do you have that give credence to the idea that you have the capacity to help the school achieve this vision?

6. Craft a vision statement by synthesizing your responses to Questions 1–5 above.

3. Leading With Inspiration

A story is a fact, wrapped in an emotion that compels us to take an action that transforms our world.

—RICHARD MAXWELL AND ROBERT DICKMAN

The Elements of Persuasion

PURPOSE

It is up to the school leader to help make sense of what people are experiencing, and to frame it in a way that empowers staff to be patient and persistent while waiting for the results of their efforts to become manifest. One of the most powerful tools effective leaders have to make sense of the current situation and link it to the school's vision and values is storytelling. A leadership narrative can provide interpretive insights that shape how people think, feel, and ultimately act. A great story becomes an adaptive metaphor that establishes where we are now, where we are headed, and what qualities will be needed for us to meet the challenges to reach our shared goals.

PROCEDURE

1. Complete the questions contained on the *Using Stories To Inspire Change Worksheet.*
2. After you have answered the questions on the worksheet, prepare a two-minute narrative that uses your personal story to engage the hearts and minds of your audience and persuades them to embrace your vision and/or call to action.
3. Practice telling your story to a colleague, and ask for feedback: What lesson did he or she learn from hearing your story? Was it relevant? Was it meaningful? What aspects of the story worked particularly well? How could it be improved?
4. Refine your narrative based on the feedback.
5. Seek out opportunities to incorporate your story into a meeting with staff, students, and families.

Using Stories to Inspire Change Worksheet

> *Every great leader is a great storyteller*
>
> —HOWARD GARDNER

1. Recall a time in your life that might be called a "transformational experience." Specifically, what happened that led you to want to become a teacher, or an educator, or a leader?

2. When was it?

3. Where were you?

4. Who else was there?

5. What actually happened?

6. What did you hear?

7. What did you see?

8. What did you do?

Using Stories to Inspire Change Worksheet, *continued*

9. What did you feel?

10. What did you think?

11. What was there about this experience that touched you, moved you, inspired you, challenged you, and motivated you to eventually become a school leader?

12. What was true about you before you had this experience?

13. How did you change in positive ways after this experience?

14. In what ways has this experience contributed to making you the right leader for this school at this time?

15. If you were to relate this experience to your staff, what would you want them to take away from it? What would you like them to think, feel, or do as a result of having heard your story?

16. If you were to relate this experience to your students, what would you want them to take away from it? What would you like them to think, feel, or do as a result of having heard your story?

4. Leading With Responsibility

*Between stimulus and response there is a space. In that
space is our power to choose our response. In our
response lies our growth and our freedom.*

—VIKTOR E. FRANKL

PURPOSE

In a communication skills workshop for couples that I conducted a while ago, a married couple very realistically demonstrated to the group their dysfunctional communication pattern. After much heated debate, the husband said to his wife, "If only you would stop repeating everything over and over again, then I could hear you." Her response: "If only you would hear me the first time, I wouldn't have to repeat myself over and over again."

They were both frustrated by their inability to communicate, but since they saw the other as being the source of the problem, they felt the only solution was to wait for the other to change. Were they able to accept personal responsibility for the situation, then the wife could have focused on changing her speaking behavior, realizing that repeating things didn't work. The husband could have focused on his listening behavior, realizing that tuning out didn't work. If both of them were at least as committed to making the relationship work as they were committed to making each other wrong, they could have broken through the stalemate situation in which they found themselves.

While there may be some payoff—not looking bad, not feeling guilty, not taking the blame—in locating the source of the problem in someone else, the cost of this irresponsible thinking and behavior is that it leaves you powerless to do anything to improve the situation.

Responsibility starts with the awareness that you are the source of your experience. Events happen, but what these events mean to you depends on what significance you give them. It's true that heavy clouds in December probably mean it will snow, but whether a major snowstorm is experienced by you as a blessing or a curse depends on whether it means you get to go skiing this week, or if it means you have to get up early to shovel the driveway in order to make it to work on time. The snow did not cause you to react one way or the other. Your point of view about the snow determined how you felt. Change your point of view and you transform your experience.

I like to use the term "radical responsibility" in order to emphasize the point that even though there are circumstances that are beyond your control, how you experience those circumstances is within your power to determine. Hence, you are personally responsible for your experience of everything that happens in your life.

Given that you are in a leadership position in your school, it is particularly important that you embrace this attitude of "radical responsibility." Schools, as with most organizations, are often plagued with CYA (Cover Your Assets) syndrome, where each individual and group point the finger of blame at another person or part of the organization. Parents blame the administrators, administrators blame the teachers, teachers blame the students, and students blame the dog that ate their homework.

The point is that until you take responsibility for your role as a leader, no one else will see you as someone who can provide direction, harness resources, and deliver the results that are needed. Self-confidence inspires confidence in others. By modeling "radical responsibility," you can help shape a culture where every member of the school community is encouraged to accept personal responsibility for doing his or her part to create an effective learning environment.

Guidelines for Practicing Radical Responsibility

Here are some things to get you started with the complex task of taking radical responsibility:

> *Rule 1: Responsibility Is Fact Finding Not Fault Finding.*   When something doesn't go as expected, ask, what happened? The point isn't to blame yourself or find fault in someone else, but rather to analyze the situation objectively to determine what factors led to the unintended outcome. What's done is done. You can't go back in time to correct what didn't work. So keep the focus on what could be done better next time.

> *Rule 2: Responsibility Is Acting Purposefully.*   Be clear about the school's mission. Don't lose sight of the school's core values. Create a vision of what's possible. Articulate the goal, objective, and intended result. Plan your day around accomplishing what matters, and direct your attention and actions toward accomplishing these.

> *Rule 3: Responsibility Is the Ability to Respond Appropriately.*   In the process of implementing your goals, "stuff happens." Successful leaders anticipate potential problems, develop contingency plans, and view obstacles as evidence that progress is being made. Their commitment to achieving the goal enables them to persevere, whereas people who are not successful in accomplishing their goals generally drop out and give up because they allow the obstacles to become excuses for why they can't meet a goal.

> *Rule 4: Responsibility Is Using Language that Connotes Power.*   The language we use to describe our experience reveals the context within which we are interpreting the events. In turn, language can be used to shape our perception of reality. For instance, if I say, "You make me angry when you don't take my ideas seriously," I am denying my responsibility for my own feelings. Compare that with this statement: "I feel angry when it appears to me that you are not taking

my ideas seriously." In this second instance, I am taking responsibility—that is, *response ability*—acknowledging that my ability to respond to circumstances is within my control. Using "I" statements makes it clear that I am speaking from my experience, and it allows for others to have their own experience of the situation, which may be different from mine.

Avoid weak words such as "I'll try" or "I hope," which suggest you are not totally committed or totally convinced of your ability to accomplish something. If I were looking to delegate a really important task that needs to be completed by a particular time, I would choose someone who can commit to deliver the result over a person who says, "I will *try* to get it done but I'm really busy right now," or "I *hope* to be able to finish it on time depending on how much work is involved."

Rule 5: Responsibility Is Encouraging Others to Take Appropriate Action. Whining and complaining about a problem is not going to solve it. Proposing the question "So what are you going to do about it?" is a good way to get someone focused on taking action to correct the situation.

When others come to you with a complaint about a co-worker, ask if they have talked directly to the person with whom they are having the problem. Listening to people vent may be useful to help them get clear on the issue they are having, but it won't solve it. If you are not the appropriate person to take action on this, then direct them to take their complaint to someone who can do something about it.

Rule 6: Responsibility Is an Internal Sense of Being Empowered to Act.   Taken to the next step, **radical accountability** makes public your commitment to implement your goals, by publishing the specific objectives by which success will be measured, and holding yourself and your team accountable for meeting these objectives. So here is your opportunity to practice radical responsibility by letting the members of your school community know what goals you have set for yourself.

PROCEDURE

1. Take the learning goals that you identified in the first activity and translate them into BOLD goals by using the *BOLD Goals Worksheet.*
2. Post your BOLD goal on a bulletin board inside your office, classroom, or staff room, and let your colleagues know that you intend to hold yourself accountable for this goal, and that you encourage their feedback as to whether or not they are observing your progress.

A **BOLD** goal is one that is **B**ig enough to be a stretch, **O**bjectively measurable, **L**inked to your school improvement plan or district strategic plan, and **D**ate-specific.

BOLD Goals Worksheet

> **B—Big enough to be a stretch**
>
> **O—Objectively measurable**
>
> **L—Linked to your school improvement plan or district strategic plan**
>
> **D—Date-specific**

1. Start with one of the learning goals you set based on the *Leadership Learning Outcomes Worksheet*. For example,

> *My goal is to increase my understanding of communication styles, and to practice ways of modifying my approach to working with different people so that I can be a more effective communicator.*

> *Your Goal:*

2. To be BOLD, it needs to be Big—big enough to be a stretch. Is the goal—as written— a big enough challenge? How might it read if it were a stretch goal? For example,

> *My goal is to increase my understanding of communication styles, and to practice ways of modifying my approach to working with different people so that I can be a more effective communicator with everyone on the staff.*

> *Your Stretch Goal:*

3. To be BOLD, it needs to be Objectively measurable. Rewrite your goal so that it states specifically how you will measure success. For example,

> *My goal is to increase my understanding of communication styles, and to practice ways of modifying my approach to working with different people so that I can be a more effective communicator with everyone on the staff, as measured by a staff survey.*

> *Your Objectively Measureable Goal:*

(continues)

BOLD Goals Worksheet, *continued*

4. To be BOLD, it needs to be linked to your school improvement plan or district strategic plan. Find the section of the school or district's plan that relates to your goal, and rewrite it so that the connection is explicitly stated. For example,

> *Our School Improvement Plan calls for "building a connected learning community." In support of this vision, my goal is to increase my understanding of communication styles, and to practice ways of modifying my approach to working with different people so that I can be a more effective communicator with everyone on the staff, as measured by a staff survey.*

> *Your Goal Linked to District/School Plans:*

5. To be BOLD, it needs to be date-specific. Set the completion dates a month from now, and double-check that the goal is stated in a way the works within this time frame. For example,

> *Our School Improvement Plan calls for "building a connected learning community." In support of this vision, my goal is to increase my understanding of communication styles, and to practice ways of modifying my approach to working with different people so that I can be a more effective communicator with everyone on the staff. Progress will be measured by a staff survey that will indicate that every staff member observed at least one action on my part over the next 30 days that clearly demonstrated my intention to improve my communication skills.*

> *Your Date-Specific Goal:*

5. Leading With Results

*Trust yourself. Create the kind of self that you will be
happy to live with all your life. Make the most of
yourself by fanning the tiny, inner sparks of possibility
into flames of achievement.*

—Golda Meir

PURPOSE

One recent survey highlighted the importance of trust between administrators and teachers and found it to be strongly correlated with teacher turnover.[2] Among the attributes associated with trust were: the communication of clear expectations to parents and students, a shared vision among faculty, consistent administrative support for teachers, and processes for group decision making and problem solving.

Trust can't be built in a day. It takes consistent behavior over time for others to come to trust that you are ethical and fair, and that you can be counted on to deliver what you promise. The purpose of this activity is to strengthen the trust that exists between you and your colleagues by inviting you to view yourself from their perspective.

To support you in taking effective action, the procedure is structured around the four steps of Plan-Do-Study-Act (PDSA). You may be familiar with the PDSA cycle made popular by Dr. W. Edwards Deming.[3] Many school districts use it as an integral tool in their school improvement programs. In northwestern Chicago, for example, District 15, which serves 12,000 students, applied the PDSA cycle to address student achievement.[4]

In the spring of 2008, eight of its schools had failed to meet adequate yearly progress (AYP) for reading. A team of principals and other district leaders was formed to tackle the problem. The team analyzed test scores and discovered that the district's intervention programs weren't working. It developed a placement matrix to guide principals and staff to the most appropriate intervention program for a student's specific learning needs.

The team also realized that the key to improving student learning was more instructional time with at-risk students. It researched and benchmarked other schools' extended day programs, then used the PDSA process and quality tools to develop and launch their own in a few months. Reading scores improved dramatically: 17 of the district's 19 schools achieved AYP on the 2009 tests.

Once you have taken advantage of using this model as a tool for your own professional development, you could consider other applications at your school site.

Plan-Do-Study-Act
(PDSA Cycle)

PROCEDURE: PART ONE

1. Imagine that you are in a school leadership position and your school district has hired an educational consulting firm to evaluate the effectiveness of school leaders. Unknown to you, one of the consultants has been working undercover as a teacher's aide in order to get experience firsthand of how much trust exists between you and the teachers at your school. After three months of observing your interactions with staff, parents, and students, the consultant has prepared his or her report using the evaluation form provided here.

2. Fill in the *School Leader Evaluation Form Worksheet* by writing in the observations you would expect the consultant to share about you with your superintendent.

School Leader Evaluation Form Worksheet

1. How would you rate the degree of trust that exists between the teachers and the school leader?

   List three things you observed the school leader doing that increased trust among staff.

   List three things you observed the school leader doing that decreased trust among staff.

   If asked to list the school leader's core values, what attributes would staff mention most often?

   Give an example of something the school leader does on a consistent basis that helps reinforce his or her commitment to these core values.

School Leader Evaluation Form Worksheet, *continued*

2. How well does the school leader communicate clear expectations to parents and students?

   Give an example of how he or she does this.

3. How well does the school leader nurture a shared vision among faculty?

   Give an example of how he or she does this.

4. How well does the school leader demonstrate consistent administrative support for teachers?

   Give an example of how he or she does this.

5. How well does the school leader engage staff in group decision-making and problem-solving processes?

   Give an example of how he or she does this.

6. Is the school leader perceived as being effective? Is he or she trusted to get things done?

   Give an example of what staff would point to as evidence of this.

7. Is the school leader perceived as being ethical? Is he or she trusted to do the right thing?

   Give an example of what staff would point to as evidence of this.

PROCEDURE: PART TWO

Plan

1. Based on what you learned from completing the *School Leader Evaluation Form Worksheet*, develop a plan for what you will do to build greater confidence in your leadership among your school community.
2. Select a few key areas of focus, for example, identifying three ways that you could be more consistent in demonstrating support for teachers.
3. Give the *Giving Constructive Feedback Survey Worksheet* to your colleagues, and invite them to submit their feedback to you in writing—signed or anonymously, or in person. Make it clear that this is voluntary, and that—while you would appreciate hearing from everyone—there will be no negative consequences for anyone who does or does not submit feedback.
4. Use your colleagues' feedback to help develop your plan. Use the number of staff members who are willing to submit feedback as an indication of the degree of trust they feel with you.

Do

5. For the next 30 days, implement your plan to do the things you've identified as ways of building greater confidence in your leadership among your school community.

Study

6. At the end of the time period, give another copy of the *Giving Constructive Feedback Staff Survey Worksheet* to your staff, and once again invite them to submit their feedback to you in writing—signed or anonymously, or in person. Reiterate that this is voluntary, and that—while you would appreciate hearing from everyone—there will be no negative consequences for anyone who does or does not submit feedback.
7. Use this feedback to make any modifications to your plan. Use the number of staff members who are willing to submit feedback as an indication of the degree of trust they feel with you. It would be safe to assume that if you were successful in building confidence with staff over the past 30 days, more of them would be comfortable providing you with feedback, and the number who met with you would be greater, as would those who signed their feedback forms rather than submitted them anonymously.

Act

8. With a better sense of what actions are working with staff, implement your improved plan.
9. After 60 days, complete the *School Leader Evaluation Form* again, and acknowledge the progress you have made toward being a more effective school leader.

Giving Constructive Feedback Staff Survey

Purpose

In an effort to continuously improve my leadership effectiveness, I am inviting you to give me feedback so that I can better serve you and, ultimately, our students. You may complete this form and sign it, or submit it anonymously. If you would prefer to discuss your feedback with me personally, I would welcome the opportunity to meet with you.

Please rate my leadership effectiveness on the following measures using this 5-point scale

1 = Not effective, 2 = Slightly effective, 3 = Moderately effective, 4 = Very effective, 5 = Exceptionally effective

How would you rate my effectiveness in building trust and confidence with the staff?
1. _____   2. _____   3. _____   4. _____   5. _____

How would you rate my effectiveness in communicating clear expectations to parents and students?
1. _____   2. _____   3. _____   4. _____   5. _____

How would you rate my effectiveness in nurturing a shared vision among the school community?
1. _____   2. _____   3. _____   4. _____   5. _____

How would you rate my effectiveness in providing consistent support to teachers?
1. _____   2. _____   3. _____   4. _____   5. _____

How would you rate my effectiveness in engaging staff in group decision making?
1. _____   2. _____   3. _____   4. _____   5. _____

How would you rate my overall effectiveness?
1. _____   2. _____   3. _____   4. _____   5. _____

Comments:

6. Leading With Values

*The act of acting morally is behaving as if
everything we do matters.*

—GLORIA STEINEM

PURPOSE

As was explored in the previous section, people trust leaders who are effective in accomplishing results that matter to them. Another important dimension of trust is based on having confidence that the person in a position of leadership is operating from a consistent set of values that are transparent and predictable. In one study, when teachers were asked their view of which of the professional administrative standards they thought were most important, they chose ethical leadership.[5] In fact, this ranked even higher than instructional leadership, which was the standard that administrators viewed as most important.

Given the increasing importance of ethics as a function of educational leadership, the use of case studies has gained wide recognition and acceptance as an effective approach to engaging school leaders in clarifying their values and applying ethical principles to resolving issues in a manner that builds trust within the school community.

The purpose of this activity is to build your knowledge and skills in ethical decision making. The case studies included here raise the kinds of ethical issues principals reported as having to deal with most frequently as well as being the most troublesome.

PROCEDURE

1. Read the first of the case studies.[6]
2. Reflect on the situation described.
3. Decide on the best course of action that the school leader should take in this situation.
4. Examine the reasons why you think this is the best course of action.
5. State what underlying values are the bases for your reasoning that this is the best choice.
6. Discuss this first case study with a colleague or in a small group of other school leaders.

7. Repeat this process with the other five case studies.
8. Finally, summarize the ethical framework/consistent value structure revealed by how you approached resolving the issues raised in the six case studies.

CASE STUDIES

Leading With Values

CIRCUMSTANCES INVOLVING STUDENTS

Case Study 1

Imagine you are the principal of a regional vocational high school.

One of your teachers told five girls not to speak Spanish among themselves in her class. The teacher, who doesn't speak Spanish herself, claims that she had a right to make this request because the girls were being disruptive. "I'm responsible for classroom management," says Ms. Ross, "and if I can't understand what the students are saying to each other about other students, then I can't ensure that the class is safe for all students and free from ethnic and other slurs."

But 16-year-old Maria Lopez asserts that she and her friends were simply chatting in Spanish and laughing as other students were permitted to do in English. The Mexican American girl says the teacher told them it was "rude" for them to speak Spanish because others in the class couldn't understand them.

Is this an issue of respecting diversity, of school safety, and/or of demonstrating administrative support for a faculty member? How do you think this should be resolved?

Case Study 2

Imagine you are the principal of an elementary school with close to 500 students preK–5th grade in a large metropolitan area that is one of the most culturally diverse counties in the nation.

One of the school counselors has been counseling a fifth-grader who has exhibited some indicators associated with individuals who may be suicidal. The eleven-year-old complained to the counselor about constantly being bullied by other students who called him gay, ugly, and "the virgin" because he was from the Virgin Islands.

The counselor is unsure of whether the student's behavior rises to the point that the student should be considered potentially at risk for suicide, and whether to inform his parents. The counselor notifies you of her concern, and reminds you that this information was communicated in a counseling session in which the student expected that he would have privacy, and he believed that the counselor would keep the information confidential.

Does the parents' right to know supersede the confidentiality concern of the counselor? Would addressing student bullying on a schoolwide basis make this student feel more or less comfortable? What appropriate actions will you take?

CIRCUMSTANCES INVOLVING STAFF

Case Study 3

Imagine you are the principal at a high school that offers a senior calculus class that cannot accommodate all the students who wish to take it. The teacher of the class, Mr. Tweten, is observed by a fellow teacher, Ms. Kelly, reviewing the records of all students who are juniors who have expressed an interest in taking the class the next academic year. When Ms. Kelly asks Mr. Tweten what he is doing, he explains that he selects the students who will be allowed to take his class based on their math score on an aptitude test all students take at the beginning of their junior year.

Mr. Tweten explains that in the past he had also tried to consider grades, motivation, diversity, and other factors in selecting students, but that the process has become too time-consuming, so now he selects students based only on their math aptitude scores. He insists that he gets the best students in the class through using the test scores as the only criterion for admission.

Ms. Kelly reminds him that the Educational Testing Service has taken a strong stand that aptitude scores should not be the sole criterion for entry into academic programs, but Mr. Tweten insists he does not have time to review other factors. Ms. Kelly wonders whether the matter should be brought to your attention but she also does not want to upset the math teacher. She decides that oversight of his selection process is not her responsibility. She does, however, mention it to one of the parents whose daughter is not likely to get into Mr. Tweten's class, and this parent contacts you.

Do you empathize with the math teacher because recent budget cutbacks have increased everyone's workload? Is it important to you that teachers follow best practices in terms of considering other factors besides aptitude tests in the student selection process? Are you upset that the other teacher did not come to you directly with her concern? How do you deal with this situation?

Case Study 4

Imagine you are the principal of a K–8 charter school, the Compass Leadership Academy. You take your role as instructional leader very seriously, and you pride yourself in the amount of time you spend visiting classrooms to observe teacher effectiveness.

Mr. Baker, a seventh-grade teacher, is very popular with the students, and every time you observed his class, you were impressed with the fact that all the students actively participated in class discussions. It has been brought to your attention that Mr. Baker has made a deal with his students. He explained to them how important it is to him that the principal view him as an excellent teacher, and that one of the main ways that the principal measures teacher effectiveness is by student engagement. So, Mr. Baker apparently told the students that when the principal is in the room, he expected all students to raise their hands every time. The deal is that if they know the answer, they are to raise their right hand, and he would call on them. If they did not know the answer, they were to raise their left hand, and that way he would know not to call on them. In a sense, all the students were participating albeit, participating in putting one over on you.

You were informed of this alleged scheme by Mrs. Dee, another teacher who has made it clear that she is not fond of Mr. Baker. She has complained that being a teacher is not a popularity contest, and that being liked by students should not be confused with being a good teacher.

What are the leadership issues involved, and how will you address this situation?

CIRCUMSTANCES INVOLVING EXTERNAL RELATIONS

Case Study 5

Imagine you are the principal of Harbor Way High School located in a community that takes its sports teams very seriously.

One of your students, Matt Brenner, the captain on the swim team and winner of the Coach's Award for being the team's most inspirational member, is under pressure from his father to run for Student Council president. According to the constitution of the Student Council, to run for office, a student must maintain a 3.0 grade point average. Unfortunately, Matt's GPA is 2.7. His father doesn't think this should disqualify him, and he has been lobbying the coach, teachers, students, and other parents to convince you to make an exception in this case.

You've known Matt's family for years, and you actually think he would make an excellent Student Council president. However, the grade point average rule exists for a good reason.

Does the fact that the student's father is trying to pressure you to bend the rules make your decision harder, easier, or have no bearing on how you will act? What will you do to resolve this matter in a fair and just manner?

Case Study 6

Imagine you are a new principal at a suburban elementary school. A parent at your school, Mrs. Spreyer, acting in her official capacity as the president of the PTA, sent you a letter welcoming you to Live Oak. After her warm words of support, her tone in the letter shifts to that of a concerned parent.

Her daughter Joyce has been assigned to Mrs. Pearson's class, and Mrs. Spreyer is none too happy about it. Mrs. Spreyer indicates that because Mrs. Pearson is young and not very experienced, she is not the right teacher for Joyce. The other fourth-grade teacher, Dr. Leon, has a lot more teaching experience and, in Mrs. Spreyer's opinion, would be better able to meet the needs of a child as intelligent and gifted as her daughter. Therefore, she is requesting that you reassign Joyce to Dr. Leon's class.

What is the school policy on transferring students to a different class? Is it more important to respect the parent's wishes—especially given her position of power at the school, or to demonstrate a vote of confidence in your new teacher whom you really do trust to do a good job? Would the student be better served by remaining in the class to which she was assigned rather than having to start over with a different teacher and new classmates? Given that this is your first year as a principal at this school, what action on your part will earn you the greatest confidence in your leadership ability? How will you respond to Mrs. Spreyer's request? ■

7. Leading With Consistency

When all else fails, read the instructions.

—Cahn's Axiom

PURPOSE

Wouldn't it be great if the operating instructions for all the important aspects of enjoying a happy and successful life were made clear upfront? In some situations, this is the case. You buy a new car, an HDTV, or an iPod, and an owner's manual provides you with the necessary information you need to get it to work properly. So, one category of operating instructions is *mechanical*.

In order to be useful, operating instructions governing mechanical or electronic devices need to work in a consistent manner. Once you learn how to access your e-mails, you should be able to follow the same procedure each time. If the instructions were random and different every time, you would probably give up in frustration. So, one operating instruction about operating instructions is that they need to be consistent in order to be useful.

A second category of operating instructions is *natural*, of which gravity is an excellent example. Gravity has great consistency. If you were to get up on top of a building and jump off, you would come down. If you were foolish enough to do it a second time, you would come down. Get on top of a building, jump off, and change your mind as you begin to descend; you would still come down. Jump off a building, and blame someone else; you would still come down. See the beauty of it? So, mechanical and natural operating instructions are fairly easy to work with because their consistency makes the outcome predictable.

Gravity helps demonstrate that there is a correlation between the quality of your life and your willingness to be responsible for operating instructions. If you keep jumping off buildings, the quality of your life will be diminished. This is also true with instructions related to mechanical or electronic devices. The iPod does not care whether you get to listen to music or not. If you want the iPod to work, you need to be responsible for following the instructions.

A third category of operating instructions is *social*. Unlike the others we've mentioned, social operating instructions are not always consistent. They tend to be approximations. Not everyone behaves in the same way. How one person processes information is not necessarily how everyone does. What motivates some people doesn't motivate others. What works in some families or cultures doesn't work in others. Even though these can be more complicated, they are no less real, and no less important to the quality of your life.

If you want your life to flow more smoothly, discover what the operating instructions are, and learn to be responsible for making things work for you. No one is making you or forcing you to do something you don't want to do. The extent to which you struggle and resist, and make things difficult for yourself, is up to you. The next time you find yourself being less than fully effective, you might want to take a step back and ask yourself, what operating instructions might be applicable in this situation?

PROCEDURE

1. Imagine if when you started a new job, your supervisor gave you a handout labeled, *"MY OPERATING INSTRUCTIONS: How to work with me so it works for you."* Well, here is a chance for you to define your own operating instructions. Think about your answers to the questions on the following worksheet, and consider how much of this would be useful information for you to share with the other members of your school community.

2. Now summarize your responses to these questions into a set of operating instructions on the *Articulating Your Own Operating Instructions Worksheet*, which could be used to inform people how they can work with you most successfully. Also see the *Sample Operating Instructions* at the end of this section for guidelines that apply to all education professionals.

Articulating Your Own Operating Instructions Worksheet

Motivation

What do you like best about working here?

What parts of your job do you find most satisfying?

(*continues*)

Articulating Your Own Operating Instructions Worksheet, *continued*

What would make you consider working somewhere else?

What are your career goals?

What is your number one priority in the next six months?

Communication

How do you prefer to get information (e.g., e-mail, telephone, in person, in writing, at formal meetings, etc.)?

Do you prefer concrete, specific, step-by-step instructions, or general, big-picture guidelines?

Under what circumstances are you open to feedback?

How do you handle conflict?

Work Style

Do you prefer to work alone, or in groups?

Articulating Your Own Operating Instructions Worksheet, *continued*

Do you prefer solving problems one-on-one, or in a group setting?

Do you prefer to work in a structured environment where rules are clear, or in a relaxed environment where rules are flexible?

What are your strengths?

What are your weaknesses?

Delegation/Decision Making

How often do you want to be updated?

When colleagues are unclear about how to proceed on a project, do you prefer that they ask you questions, or would you rather have them figure it out their own?

How do you deal with mistakes when they are made?

When do you involve people in the decision-making process?

Performance

What are your performance goals?

What is your definition of a top performer?

(*continues*)

Articulating Your Own Operating Instructions Worksheet, *continued*

How do you evaluate performance?

How do you express satisfaction?

How do others know when they are not meeting your expectations?

Personality Style

Do you prefer socializing with co-workers, or getting down to business?

Are you more idealistic or pragmatic?

How would you describe your sense of humor?

Is it easier for you to grant permission, or grant forgiveness?

Do you have any idiosyncrasies that people should know about?

Articulating Your Own Operating Instructions Worksheet, *continued*

How-I-Like-to-be-Managed Style

Do you prefer a hands-on or hands-off manager?

Do you prefer a people person or a process person?

Under what conditions do you respect your manager?

Under what conditions do you trust your manager?

Under what conditions do you enjoy working with your manager?

Pet Peeves

What kinds of things drive you crazy?

Have you ever gotten really angry at work, and what triggered it?

What else do people need to know about you in order for them to work with you effectively?

Sample Operating Instructions

---

1. Promoting student achievement is our number 1 priority. If I do anything that makes it more difficult for you to do your job, I expect you to tell me about it.
2. If you have a problem with me, I would appreciate the courtesy of your talking with me about it in person so that we can clear it up.
3. I work best with people who respect my time by being prepared and organized.
4. I base my decisions on facts and figures, and do not respond well to emotional appeals.
5. I hate surprises. I prefer to be proactive rather than reactive. I need you to anticipate potential problems and keep me informed when there is still time for me to get out in front of the issue.
6. I'm not as good as I would like to be in giving positive feedback. You have my permission to remind me to recognize your accomplishments.

I am open to receiving feedback, provided it is done respectfully and in private.

In Conclusion

The main point to remember from this first part of the book is that people trust and have confidence in leaders who demonstrate clarity, concern, and competence.

- Clarity—Are you able to articulate a clear and inspiring vision? Is it transparently clear what you value, and do you apply these values consistently?
- Concern—Do you care about what matters most to others? Do you know what they need to succeed, and do you provide it?
- Competence—Do you deliver on what you promise? Do you get things done?

PART TWO

TO LEAD IS TO LISTEN— COMMUNICATION SKILLS
6 Tools to Enhance Communication

The colossal misunderstanding of our time is the assumption that insight will work with people who are unmotivated to change. Communication does not depend on syntax, or eloquence, or rhetoric, or articulation, but on the emotional context in which the message is being heard. People can only hear you when they are moving toward you, and they are not likely to when your words are pursuing them. Even the choicest words lose their power when they are used to overpower. Attitudes are the real figures of speech.

—EDWIN H. FRIEDMAN

If you maintained a time log for the next two weeks where you kept track of all your work-related activities in 15-minute increments, what would you discover about what a school leader actually does? What percentage of your time would you say is spent in some form of communication: speaking, listening, writing, and/or reading? If you include talking to yourself in the category of communication, then how much time is left for activities that do not include some type of communication? Suffice it to say that effective communication skills are absolutely essential to your success. In my opinion, education *is* communication.

Communication has three dimensions: **content**, which is *what* you say; **process**, which is *how* you say it; and **context**, which is *who* you are, *to whom* you are speaking, *where*, *when*, and *why*. Obviously, a lot is happening in the context dimension. When a breakdown in communication occurs, most often it is a function of differences in context.

Features of organizational context, such as geographic location (urban, suburban, or rural), the size of the school and of the district, and the level of schooling (elementary or secondary), all have important implications. School leaders in a small elementary school, for example, are more likely to have a more direct instructional leadership role than a leader in a large secondary school who would probably rely on department heads to work more closely with teachers.

In this section, you will consider the significance of context and how Dedicated Listening is essential to understanding someone else's frame of reference, and to building common ground of shared meaning. Research shows that not only is it identified as a necessary job skill by senior executives in many fields, but it is also mentioned more often than any other skill including managerial ability and technical competence.

After we have a better grasp of the power of context in communication, we will examine one key aspect of the communication process, which involves the recognition of different communication styles. The idea of dividing human behavior into temperaments or personality types is certainly not new. Although it may date back to ancient Egypt or Mesopotamia, it was around 400 B.C. when Hippocrates created his system for dividing human moods, emotions, and behaviors into "four humors."

The lessons in this section will help you learn how to adapt your delivery so that your communication produces the result you intended. You will also gain insights into how to improve relationships with members of your team and the community, including those with whom you've had difficulty in the past. The group activities included here can be used with your colleagues and peers or book study group, or on-site with you staff or School Improvement Team.

1. Recognizing the Difference Between Content and Context

A wise man, the wonder of his age, taught his disciples from a seemingly inexhaustible store of wisdom. He attributed all his knowledge to a thick tome which was kept in a place of honor in his room. The sage would allow nobody to open the volume.

When he died, those who had surrounded him, regarding themselves as his heirs, ran to open the book, anxious to possess what it contained. They were surprised, confused and disappointed when they found that there was writing on only one page. They became even more bewildered and then annoyed when they tried to penetrate the meaning of the phrase which met their eyes. It was: "When you realize the difference between the container and the content, you will have knowledge."

—INDRIES SHAH

PURPOSE

I often tell this Sufi story at the beginning of my communication skills workshop because I find it to be a good way of introducing the importance of **context** in being able to accurately grasp the meaning of someone's communication. In terms of communication, content is what you say and the container is the context or the frame or reference, which establishes the meaning of the communication. That's why when you take something out of context, you often distort its meaning. To be an effective communicator, you must pay attention to context.

One's context is the body of beliefs that make up your worldview, and it tends to shape and filter your perception in such a way that you are apt to view circumstances in ways that are compatible with your context, and disagree with or discard any evidence that conflicts with your beliefs. This tendency to seek or interpret evidence in ways that are partial to existing beliefs, expectations, or a hypothesis in hand is referred to as "confirmation bias" in the psychological literature.

Let me illustrate the importance of context by using a personal example. After a presentation I gave to some 300 or so parents, I was touched by one of the mothers who came up to me after the talk to thank me for my comments. She said she gained a lot of value from my ideas and went on to say that it was clear to her that I "had a personal relationship with the Lord." There was no reference to religion in my presentation, yet from her viewpoint, something I said or didn't say led her to assume I was a born-again Christian.

Later that evening when I was reading some written evaluations of my presentation, I was struck by this comment: "Dr. Siccone and his secular-humanistic philosophy shouldn't be allowed in our schools." In this case, something I said or didn't say led this parent to assume I was an atheist. That two people in the same audience heard two completely opposite messages was particularly intriguing. How is this possible?

Obviously, each parent was listening to my words and hearing them from within their own frame-of-reference, their context. Taking something out of context—by mistake or by deliberately attempting to deceive—is to remove the statement from its original setting or frame of reference, thereby distorting its meaning. Virtually all miscommunication can be traced to differences in context. At my parent presentation, I spoke about self-esteem from my context and the parents heard what they heard in their contexts.

The purpose of this activity is to identify important aspects of your "context" so that you can be more aware of how your worldview may be influencing your perception and interpretation of events, and so others will have a better sense of where you are coming from.

PROCEDURE

1. Make a list of life experiences that have shaped your context/worldview. Consider childhood experiences, family, friends, relationships, places where you've lived, education, socioeconomic situation, culture, race, ethnicity, work experience, health issues, religion, politics, etc.
2. Whom do you know who has exactly the same context as yours? (Sorry for the trick question. Just wanted to make the point that it is amazing that we communicate as well as we do, given that each of us has our own unique context within which we interpret what is being said.)
3. Select one of your life experiences that has had a profound influence on your context. Complete the following statements:

    Given my life experience, my context includes (insert a core belief, value, or assumption) _____

    _____

    Therefore, I tend to (insert an expectation, perception, or interpretation)

    _____

    As a consequence, I can have difficulty understanding, respecting, or listening to someone who _____

    _____

For example,

> Given my life experience, my context includes a philosophy of "radical responsibility" that posits that we create our own experience of reality.
>
> Therefore, I tend to expect people to take ownership for what works or doesn't work in their lives.
>
> As a consequence, I can have difficulty listening to people who act like victims of their circumstances.

4. Repeat this exercise with two other context-shaping life experiences.

1. Recognizing the Difference Between Content and Context

Part Two: Group Activity

There are no facts, only interpretations.

—Friedrich Nietzsche

PURPOSE

Here is a similar activity to be done in a group setting. It is a great team-building exercise that would work well in professional educator workshops, or courses.

PROCEDURE

1. Using an easel, flip chart, or large piece of paper, divide the page in thirds by drawing two lines horizontally across the paper. Label the top third "past," the middle third, "present," and the bottom third, "future."
2. Using a number of different-colored markers, draw pictures, visual images, and/or icons to represent important elements of your "context," as follows:
   - Past: Draw three to five images representing past experiences that were most important in shaping your worldview.
   - Present: Draw three to five images representing things (e.g., people, activities, interests, etc.) in your present life that are most important to you right now.
   - Future: Draw three to five images representing goals, ambitions, aspirations that you have for the future.
3. After you have completed this exercise, share your *Putting Me in Context* drawing with other members of the team, and discuss how past experiences, present priorities, and future goals influence how you view your role as a school leader or future leader. Discussing this with someone will help you better understand yourself and your motivations. It will also help your colleagues get a better sense of "where you're coming from" and how to interpret your words and actions.

2. Being a Dedicated Listener

To listen well is as powerful a means of influence as to talk well, and is as essential to all true conversation.

—CHINESE PROVERB

Ear   Eyes

Heart

Listening

PURPOSE

The Chinese character for the word "listening" includes the symbols for the eyes, ears, and heart reflecting the multidimensional aspects of listening.

The concept of "active listening" is certainly not new. In fact, the term was coined in 1957 by Carl Rogers and Richard Farson, and made popular again 20 years later by Thomas Gordon in the book *Parent Effectiveness Training*. Other ways of discussing the idea include "mindful listening," which emphasizes the importance of being fully present in the moment, and taking the perspective of the other. "Naive listening" suggests listening without presuming to know what the other person is about to say, or assuming you know what he or she means without verifying it. "Contextual listening" is used in coaching as is "committed listener." In my couples coaching, I introduce the practice of "dedicated listener," where one person accepts full responsibility for listening to his or her partner, with the intention of accepting the other's experience without judgment. "Nonviolent communication" is another excellent model for facilitating peaceful and productive dialogue.

The fact that most of us have been exposed to some theory about the importance of Dedicated Listening skills doesn't mean that we are all sufficiently disciplined to practice these skills on an ongoing basis.

The point of listening effectively is to expand your understanding of someone else's context so that you are better able to appreciate the meaning of their communication. Given that your goal is to encourage the other person to communicate more fully and honestly, you will want to engage in behaviors—both verbal and nonverbal—that send the message that you are paying attention and interested in what the other person is saying.

For example, you can probably assume that people are listening to you when they engage in the following behaviors:

- Making eye contact
- Nodding their head
- Leaning forward
- Smiling
- Asking you to tell them more
- Restating what they are hearing
- Asking questions to confirm their understanding
- Validating your thoughts and feelings without judgment
- Not interrupting you
- Not multitasking

Some ineffective listening behaviors you might observe yourself or others doing include:

- Listening for agreement—seeking recognition that you are right
- Listening to challenge—seeking to find fault with the other's thinking
- Listening selectively—seeking to hear only what you want to hear
- Listening while distracted—seeking to get other things done
- Rehearsing in your mind what you will say when the other finishes
- Misinterpreting what the other means
- Jumping to conclusions
- Tuning out because you don't care what the other has to say, or don't want to hear it

PROCEDURE

1. Keep a listening log over the next week where you record observations about your listening skills. Use the *Listening Log Template Worksheet* to help you keep track of your listening behaviors. Four times during the course of a day (e.g., 10 a.m., 12 noon, 2 p.m., 4 p.m.), take a few minutes to note the conversations you've had over the past couple of hours, and record your listening behavior for each. Reflect on your effectiveness using the following questions:
   - How well did you listen?
   - What made it easy to listen?
   - What made it difficult to listen?
   - What would you do differently next time?

2. After keeping the log for a week, reflect on patterns of listening behaviors that are clear based on the data you've collected. Identify one listening skill you would like to improve, and practice improving this skill during the next week.

Listening Log Template Worksheet

Date/Time	Conversation	Listening Behavior	Reflection

2. Being a Dedicated Listener

Part Two: Group Activity

Listening is to hearing what reading is to seeing.

—MIKE STEWART

PURPOSE

The purpose of this activity is to apply Dedicated Listening skills to a group situation where you have limited time to come to consensus on a difficult decision. When you read through the "Have A Heart" scenario, you may wonder why you are being asked to role-play being a group of surgeons rather than being given an activity involving a group of educators. The point of using a hypothetical situation is so that the group can maintain some perspective with regard to the process and not get totally caught up in the content.

This activity has been done hundreds of times with many different types of teams, and it has consistently proven to be not only highly engaging but also very instructive. It makes a great warm-up activity for a team to use before taking on a real job-related situation that requires everyone to listen with an open mind so that they can ultimately arrive at a decision or resolution that works for everyone.

In one of my workshops, the team was about five minutes into the process of trying to decide which patient should receive the heart transplant. One of the participants proposed the idea of putting all the names of potential recipients in a hat and just picking one. His teammates assumed he wasn't taking this exercise seriously, and ignored his suggestion.

About 10 minutes later, when they were still struggling to come to consensus, the same fellow restated his position that it should be done by random selection. Once again, the rest of the group discarded what they clearly thought was an absurd idea. They had invested 15 minutes establishing criteria for evaluating the relative worth of each of the patients, and they needed to complete the process with the few minutes remaining. I intervened by reminding them of the ground rule that they needed to listen to and validate what was said before they could move on.

The self-appointed team leader repeated the lottery idea and then went on to say that while he heard the suggestion, he felt that it was not really an option. As surgeons, they had a professional duty to make a decision and leaving it to chance would be irresponsible and unethical. The person who proposed the lottery objected to that characterization. "If anything is unethical," he claimed, "it's you trying to play God by assuming you have the right to say that one person's life is more valuable than another."

It was fascinating to realize that in one person's context not choosing was unethical, and in another person's context choosing was unethical. A valuable lesson about not judging where someone else is coming from based on your own context was learned by the team in a very memorable way.

PROCEDURE

1. This activity should be done in teams of five to seven people.
2. Locate the *Dedicated Listening Guidelines "I'm All EARS."* statements and questions to review active listening skills.
3. Since the purpose of the activity is to practice Dedicated Listening, the rule is that before anyone can express an opinion, he or she must have listened to the opinion expressed by the person who spoke prior and restate what the person said in a way that acknowledges the validity of that person's point of view.
4. Everyone on the team has the right and responsibility to manage the process—both in terms of ensuring that everyone has been listened to, as well as making sure that the team arrives at a decision by the end of the 20-minute timeframe.
5. Locate the *Dedicated Listening Activity "Have A Heart" exercise.*[1]
6. Note the starting time.
7. At the end of 20 minutes, time is up.
8. Discuss what lessons were learned by doing the activity, and how these can be applied to you.

Dedicated Listening Guidelines: "I'm all EARS."

> Listening looks easy, but it's not simple. Every head is a world.
> —CUBAN PROVERB

ENCOURAGE—Here are some sample statements and open-ended questions:
- *Please tell me more.*
- *What you're saying is important to me. Please continue.*
- *Help me understand what you are saying.*

ACKNOWLEDGE—Here are some sample statements:
- *I can see your point.*
- *I can appreciate your situation.*
- *I respect your opinion on this.*

RESTATE/REFLECT—Here are some sample clarifying questions:
- *Are you saying that . . . ?*
- *Do I understand you correctly that . . . ?*

(continues)

Dedicated Listening Guidelines: "I'm all EARS.," *continued*

- *What specifically do you mean by . . .?*
- *So what you are saying is . . . and how you feel about that is . . .*

SUMMARIZE—Here are some sample statements and summarizing questions:
- *Let me see if I got this accurately, so far you've said that . . .*
- *So, as I understand it, your point is . . . Is this correct?*
- *Now that we are clear on this, may I suggest that we move on to?*

Dedicated Listening Activity "Have a Heart"

Imagine that you are a group of surgeons at a big hospital. As a committee, you must make a very important decision. There is one heart donor at this time, and there are eight patients who need a heart transplant. Your committee must decide who will receive the transplant. You have 20 minutes to arrive at a group consensus.
      (Remember to be all EARS.)

Starting Time: _____

PATIENTS:

1. An illegal immigrant who is in need of a second operation as a result of a clerical error on the part of the hospital. A heart with the wrong blood type was used during a previous transplant. There is some question as to whether she can survive another operation so soon after the first.
2. A 15-year-old pregnant woman. She is unmarried and has no other children.
3. A religious leader and community organizer who has dedicated his life to running a homeless shelter and soup kitchen that feeds thousands of people daily. His very large and politically well-connected congregation is praying for his recovery.
4. A scientist close to discovering a cure for AIDS who is HIV-positive himself. Letters of support have been received from the world AIDS community expressing their concern that were he not able to continue his work, the search for a cure would be severely hampered.
5. A high school senior, class president, who recently won a scholarship to medical school. Ever since she was a child, she has always dreamed of becoming a doctor. She would also be the first person in her large extended family to go to college.
6. A mother of three young children. She is an Iraqi widow with no other family in this country. Her husband was killed while serving as a translator for the American troops in Baghdad.
7. An 11-year-old Tibetan monk who has been anointed the reincarnated "living Buddha." He believes his mission is to teach the people of the world how to live in peace.
8. The son of a wealthy foreign businessman whose father has offered to donate 15 million dollars to the hospital's new children's ward in return for having his son placed on the top of the list of potential heart recipients.

3. Measuring Rapport by Results

*I know that you believe you understand what you think
I said, but I'm not sure you realize that what you heard
is not what I meant.*

—ROBERT MCCLOSKEY

PURPOSE

When would-be voters do not pay attention to or buy into political ads designed to get them to vote a certain way, we don't tend to blame the voter. Typically, it is the candidate and his or her handlers who are seen as having missed the mark and wasted millions of dollars in ineffective campaign spending. That is to say, it is the sender of the communication not the receiver who is responsible for its effectiveness. Likewise, if a company spends a fortune on advertising a product that no one buys, we don't blame the consumer for not listening to and being motivated to run out and make the purchase. Once again, it is the senders—the advertising communications professionals— who are responsible for not developing and delivering a compelling message.

However, when it comes to interpersonal communication, it is often the receiver of the communication who is blamed if he or she didn't listen or failed to comprehend the message correctly. The project manager tells her staff person she needs an executive summary completed by the end of the week. She gets back a 12-page report and can't believe that he thought that's what she wanted. Now because of him, she has to work the weekend to consolidate it into a two-page document.

Clearly, the meaning of your communication extends beyond what you think it means to what happens as a result of it. You can dramatically improve your effectiveness by measuring the accuracy and strength of your communication by the extent to which it actually produces what you intended. To improve your communication, ask yourself two critical questions:

1. What is the *purpose* of my communication? (Why am I telling them this, i.e., to inform, to instruct, to influence, to persuade, to motivate, to invite reflection, to spark insight?)
2. What is the *intended result* of my communication? (What do I want them to think, feel, or do as a consequence?)

PROCEDURE

1. Create some reminders using sticky notes. Print "What's my purpose?" and "What's my intended result?" on a number of pieces of note paper and stick one on your phone, another on your computer, one on your desk and the conference table. Place them anywhere you are likely to engage in important conversations. Use this technique to get yourself in the habit of framing your communication with a clear purpose and intended result.
2. Practice using this structure on a consistent basis. Make sure all meetings have an agenda that includes the purpose and intended results of the meeting.
3. Pay more attention to the results you produce through your communications. For example, if you were to send an e-mail to a group asking them to respond to you by the end of the week, note how many responses you actually receive. If it is less than expected, review your communication—content, tone, clarity, and means. Decide how it could be made clearer, stronger, and more effective. Revise your communication based on this data. Continue to monitor your communication strategies until you increase your effectiveness in achieving the results you intend.

3. Measuring Rapport by Results

Part Two: Group Activity

There are people who, instead of listening to what is being said to them, are already listening to what they are going to say themselves.

—ALBERT GUINON

PURPOSE

The theme of this section is "To Lead Is to Listen." Sometimes, however, to lead is to listen and then to move on. Being a good listener does not mean giving up your responsibility to be an effective leader who is capable of motivating people and directing projects. The purpose of this activity is to demonstrate your ability to listen to and accurately **restate** someone's point of view, to then **reassert** your own perspective, and then to **redirect** the individual or the group to take action that you deem to be appropriate.

PROCEDURE

The *Restate, Reassert, Redirect Sample Statements* provide examples of how you can acknowledge having heard someone's communication, and—without invalidating his or her perspective—provide leadership as to a next step or to a satisfactory resolution.

1. Read through the three examples to familiarize yourself with the structure of the communication.
2. Divide into teams of five to seven people.
3. As with "Have a Heart," the purpose of the activity is to practice effective listening. The rule is that before anyone can express an opinion, he or she must have listened to the opinion expressed by the person who spoke prior and restate

what the person said in a way that acknowledges the validity of that person's point of view.

4. Each team can select one member of the team to be the team leader, who will serve in a facilitative leadership role. While everyone on the team has the right and responsibility to manage the process, the team leader is particularly responsible for ensuring that the group arrives at a decision by the end of the 20-minute timeframe.
5. Locate the *Blueprint for Reform worksheet*.
6. Note the starting time.
7. Around 15 minutes into the activity, the team leader begins using the Restate, Reassert, Redirect structure to help lead the team toward coming to a recommended course of action.
8. At the end of 20 minutes, time is up.
9. Discuss what lessons were learned by doing the activity. Compare the experience of this activity to that of the earlier *Have a Heart* activity. Explore the pros and cons of having a team leader, and develop guidelines for when it would be appropriate to have someone in this role, and when it would not.

Restate, Reassert, Redirect Sample Statements

1. Restate	*I appreciate your concern about our needing to move this forward in order to stay on schedule.*
2. Reassert	*I also think that it is important that we all understand the benefits and costs of our decision.*
3. Redirect	*So, I propose that we spend another 15 minutes discussing our options so that we have consensus on how we are going to proceed.*
1. Restate	*Your point about not just getting it done but getting it done right is well taken.*
2. Reassert	*At the same time, the superintendent has made a commitment to the school board that every school in the district will begin implementing the program immediately.*
3. Redirect	*Therefore, I think that we need to move forward with the original timeline. As we implement the program, we can document issues and concerns as they arise and bring them to the attention of the superintendent.*
1. Restate	*The issue you are raising is important and needs to be addressed.*
2. Reassert	*It is also true that we already have a full agenda for this meeting.*
3. Redirect	*Let me recommend that we include your issue as the first agenda item for our next meeting.*

Blueprint for Reform Worksheet

Imagine you are members of the district's School Improvement Team on which the assistant superintendent functions as the team leader. One of the schools in the district has been underperforming for years, and the school board has asked the superintendent for a recommendation as to how to address this failing school. The superintendent has asked you to formulate a plan providing him or her with a strong rationale for the reform solution you propose. Essentially, there are four options, which are listed here along with some background information you might want to consider as you decide what to propose. The superintendent will be joining you in 20 minutes expecting to hear your decision.

Starting Time: _____

Option 1: Turnaround—replacing the school principal and at least half the staff

Background information: The school principal is a friend of the superintendent, and was handpicked by him or her for this position. This may be one of the reasons the school staff has been resistant to him or her efforts at making changes. The School Improvement Team has put lot of energy into supporting the principal's success, and replacing him or her might be seen as a failure of this team as well as of the superintendent.

Option 2: Restart—converting the school to an autonomous charter school or hiring an education management organization to run it

Background information: A vocal group of parents have been lobbying to turn this into a magnet school for students who excel in science and math. While this would appeal to a certain percentage of families that live in the district, the majority of students currently attending this school would not eligible to attend because their grade point averages in these academic areas would not meet the criteria being proposed by the parents for admission.

Option 3: Shutdown—closing a school and dispersing its students

Background information: The School Improvement Team has invested considerable time and resources recruiting, hiring, and coaching an excellent and enthusiastic group of new teachers to work at this school. While the results of this infusion of new teachers have not yet been evidenced in test scores, you all feel confident that given more time, your investment will reap rewards. If the school is closed, then the teachers with tenure will be reassigned to other schools, and the younger, more energetic staff will be let go not only at this school, but also at the other schools where the tenured teachers will be given priority.

Option 4: Transformation—replacing the principal, improving teacher effectiveness, and taking other steps for comprehensive reform

Background information: This is what was tried two years ago when the current principal was hired along with the group of new teachers. It is unclear what could be done differently this time that would make a difference. What could possibly be included in a new School Improvement Plan that would convince the board that this is the best option?

4. Learning Styles

Great communicators have an appreciation for positioning. They understand the people they're trying to reach and what they can and can't hear. They send their message in through an open door rather than trying to push it through a wall.

—JOHN KOTTER

PURPOSE

It is obvious to even the most casual observer that not everyone processes information in the same way. As an educator, you can appreciate the importance of recognizing different learning styles. Some people prefer to work alone and uninterrupted, others prefer cooperative team interaction. Analytical thinkers usually respond best to information presented in a logical, sequential, step-by-step manner. More innovative types enjoy creative brainstorming sessions where seemingly disparate ideas may trigger new insights. By adapting your communication style to meet the preference of the person you are seeking to inform or persuade, you increase the likelihood of your communication producing the result you intend.

While this information may not be new to you, it is such an essential skill that it is included here to reinforce its importance and invite new applications such as when giving feedback or dealing with difficult people.

There are any number of communication style models, many of which present essentially the same information with somewhat different labels (see Table 2.1). You are probably familiar with Myers-Briggs Type Indicator. Other popular ones include the Keirsey Temperament Sorter, DiSC assessment, Social Styles, True Colors, and the Personality Compass. Like most of the others, my adaptation divides communication style into four primary types by creating a matrix with two dimensions—low to high assertiveness, and low to high expressiveness.[2]

Assertiveness is the amount of confidence and directness a person exhibits when stating his or her opinions. People with high assertiveness are commanding and forceful. Less assertive individuals are more cautious and tentative in how they propose their ideas.

Expressiveness is the amount of comfort a person exhibits when sharing feelings and emotions. People with high expressiveness are sociable and demonstrative. Less expressive individuals are more private and self-contained.

TABLE 2.1 Communication Styles

COLLABORATIVE Low Assertive High Expressive	**CREATIVE** High Assertive High Expressive
CONSCIENTIOUS Low Assertive Low Expressive	**COMPETITIVE** High Assertive Low Expressive

COMMUNICATION STYLES

SELF-ASSESSMENT

Procedure

While all of us can relate to each of the four styles and often use aspects of each style, typically one is predominant. The first step is for you to determine which of these communication styles most accurately describes how you interact with people and projects. Complete the following self-assessment on the *Communication Styles Self-Assessment Worksheet* to gain insight into your preferred communication style.

Communication Styles Self-Assessment Worksheet

Below are four columns of communication characteristics from which you are to choose which of these best describes your preferred style. Working across each row, rate the degree to which you identify with each of the four statements by giving it a score from 0 to 10 (0 meaning you do not identify at all with this statement, and 10 meaning you identify completely with this statement). The scores across the row must add up to 10 (for example, 10, 0, 0, 0, or 1, 1, 1, 7, or 3, 2, 3, 2,—in other words, any combination of four numbers adding to 10).

I prefer to make decisions on my own based on what I think will work best given the facts of the situation. ___	I prefer to make decisions in a group setting that stimulates my creative intuition. ___	I prefer to make decisions in a collaborative manner so that everyone involved feels good about it. ___	I prefer to make decisions on my own after careful and deliberate analysis of all the data. ___
I prefer to be rewarded for the results I produce. ___	I prefer to be recognized for the way I inspire people to imagine new possibilities. ___	I prefer to be appreciated for being supportive and encouraging of people. ___	I prefer to be judged on the accuracy and thoroughness of my work. ___
I prefer to get to the point and just get things done. ___	I prefer to explore options and to adapt to the unexpected. ___	I prefer to listen to what others think and feel before I act. ___	I prefer to take things one step at a time to make sure I do it right. ___
It is important to me to accomplish what I set out to achieve. ___	It is important to me to come up with new and innovative ideas. ___	It is important to me that everyone gets along, and feels included. ___	It is important to me that we use tried and true methods, and not waste time reinventing the wheel. ___

Communication Styles Self-Assessment Worksheet, *continued*

Others may see me as too domineering, but I prefer to think of myself as an effective leader with the self-confidence to know I'm right. ___	Others may see me as too egotistical, but I prefer to think of myself as a talented person who has a right to be different. ___	Others may see me as too accommodating, but I prefer to think of myself as a peacekeeper. ___	Others may see me as too rigid, but I prefer to think of myself as the one who knows how to keep things running smoothly. ___
I believe students learn best in a competitive environment that challenges them with high performance standards. ___	I believe students learn best in a creative environment where they are free to express their unique potential. ___	I believe students learn best in a cooperative environment where they feel good about themselves and respect one another. ___	I believe students learn best in a structured environment where rules and expectations are clearly defined. ___
My motto is, "Actions speak louder than words." ___	My motto is, "Some people see things as they are and ask why? But, I dream of things that never were and ask why not?" ___	My motto is, "Together Everyone Accomplishes More." ___	My motto is, "Say what you mean and mean what you say." ___
___ **Total column 1**	___ **Total column 2**	___ **Total column 3**	___ **Total column 4**

After you have rated each of the four items across all seven rows, then total the numbers for each column.

Interpretation

If your highest column total is column 1, then your communication style is **Competitive.**

If your highest column total is column 2, then your communication style is **Creative.**

If your highest column total is column 3, then your communication style is **Collaborative.**

If your highest column total is column 4, then your communication style is **Conscientious.**

COMMUNICATION STYLES

Competitive Style

If you are a competitive-style communicator, you are probably someone who is results-oriented, motivated by accomplishments, and likes to get things done. You look for ways to get tasks or projects completed quickly, accurately, and on time.

Because you have a high degree of self-confidence, you tend to make decisions quickly, and to act without seeking the advice or approval of others. You speak authoritatively using concrete terms and focusing on facts, not feelings. Not one to engage in small talk, you like to get to the point. You say something once and then move on.

Assuming the leadership position when working in groups comes naturally to you. You enjoy competing, you like to win, and being the best is important to you.

Creative Style

If you are a creative-style communicator, you can be extremely persuasive and have the ability to inspire and motivate others. You can often speak authoritatively and convincingly even on topics for which you possess only limited knowledge.

Innovation is important to you. Starting new projects and finding new ways of doing things are fun for you. Spontaneous by nature, you tend to be a risk-taker and often make decisions based on your "gut feelings." Keeping your options open, so as not to get tied down to any one thing for too long, matters a lot to you.

You prefer working with others rather than alone, especially when you get to be the center of attention. You enjoy being recognized and rewarded for the unique contributions you make.

You are a natural visionary who dreams big, enjoys a variety of different interests, and looks for connections between ideas.

Collaborative Style

If you are a collaborative-style communicator, you probably have great "people skills." Recognized as a great listener, you work well in groups and adapt quickly and easily to other people's way of doing things. You attempt to include everyone's opinions and are known for being a great team player. A harmonious work environment is very important to your job satisfaction.

Comfortable with emotions, you prefer to have close, meaningful relationships with others. Respect and trust matter a lot to you. It is natural for you to be empathetic and to care about other people's feelings and concerns. It is hard for you to separate policies from the people who will be affected by them.

You seek to build consensus around decisions that need to be made, and strive to find win/win solutions that everyone can support. Making a difference in people's lives is a strong motivator for you.

Conscientious Style

If you are a conscientious-style communicator, you are a natural administrator—very organized and detail-oriented. Planning ahead, being well prepared, and having enough time to do the job correctly are all important to you.

Your prefer working alone rather than as part of a team. You like to concentrate on the task at hand without being interrupted. Your job satisfaction is derived from doing high-quality, accurate work. You want all relevant facts and documentation before committing to a decision. One of your pet peeves is having your time wasted by other people's disorganization, lack of planning, and incompetence.

People know if they want something done and done right, you are the person for the job, and you agree with their assessment.

4. Learning Styles

Part Two: Group Activity

*The single biggest problem in communication is the
illusion that it has taken place.*

—George Bernard Shaw

PURPOSE

The purpose of this activity is to deepen your understanding of the four different communication styles and to observe how communication styles influence how people work together to achieve a common goal.

PROCEDURE

1. Divide into teams by communication style, so that all the collaborators are on one team, all the competitors are on one team, and so forth.
2. Each team needs a blank easel page or piece of paper and some colored markers.
3. Imagine you have been invited to a statewide conference of school leaders. Each district has been asked to have its representatives come to the conference wearing a T-shirt that communicates a message you believe is essential to effective school leadership.
4. Your task is to work together as a team to come up with a design for the T-shirt that best meets this challenge. Only one design will be selected, and there are three other teams competing. You have 20 minutes to design your T-shirt and draw it on the piece of larger paper to share with the full group.
5. Someone should be assigned the task of being the moderator/timekeeper. This person makes sure everyone is on the correct team, that each team has the supplies it needs, and that everyone understands the assignment. He or she announces when to start and, at the end of 20 minutes, calls, "time is up." At that point, all teams must stop working, and post their completed T-shirt design up on the wall so that everyone can see all four designs.
6. Each team should then take a turn in describing its design and discussing the process team members went through to accomplish the task.

7. The moderator should ask questions to help find links between the T-shirt designs and the teams' communication styles. See Process Guidelines.
8. The moderator should also ask questions to help find links between the process each team used to arrive at its design solution and that team's communication style. See Process Guidelines.
9. Finally, the full group should discuss what they learned from the exercise and how they will apply it.

T-SHIRT COMPETITION

PROCESS GUIDELINES

Debriefing the designs

Creative teams tend to have the most colorful designs, and often introduce unique elements such as hoods or bracelets. They've also been known to do a black-on-black design because they are too cool to wear a typical T-shirt.

Conscientious teams tend to come up with designs that are simple and straightforward. If there is an existing district logo or motto, they might just go with what has worked in the past rather than try to "reinvent the wheel."

Collaborative teams are likely to use the word "we," may include images of people—often holding hands—as part of their design. They frequently incorporate many different ideas into their design because they want everyone on their team to be happy.

Competitive teams usually get right to the point, maybe using a list of a few words that succinctly convey what they want to communicate. Their choice of words is likely to be result-oriented goal statements.

Debriefing the process

Creative teams typically have trouble agreeing on a single design. Each team member tends to prefer his or her own ideas, and may work on the task alone rather than stick with the group process. It is not unheard of that the creative team will present a number of different designs because if it tried to get everyone to agree on one solution, it might never complete the task—at least not in the 20 minutes allotted.

Conscientious teams are likely to follow instructions including keeping track of the time. They will typically first decide how they are going to do it before taking action.

Collaborative teams may first start by giving each person an opportunity to express how he or she feels about the assignment. They are likely to ask each other a lot of questions and allow time to make sure everyone is heard. It is not unusual for collaborative teams to consider who else will be wearing the T-shirts and how they might feel about it. More often than not, the collaborative team will not finish on time.

Competitive teams just want to get the task done and move on to what's next. If someone on the team comes up with a good idea, often they will just go with it, and not spend a lot of time discussing other options. You can expect the competitive team to finish first.

5. Connecting With Style

*What is more malleable is always superior over that
which is immoveable. This is the principle of controlling
things by going along with them, of mastery through
adaptation.*

—LAO TZU

PURPOSE

With a deeper understanding of how to read someone else's communication style, let's
look at ways that you can match each of the styles for maximum effectiveness.

Adapting your communication style in order to communicate more effectively
with another is not about being dishonest or inauthentic. You are not changing
anything fundamental about yourself, your values or principles, or your goals and
objectives. Nor are you trying to fool someone or manipulate him or her by altering
your essential message. Your are merely modifying the manner or style with which you
are conveying your message so that the other person can process the information you
are presenting more easily, and comprehend your communication in terms that are
more meaningful to him or her.

PROCEDURE

1. Identify someone with whom it is critically important that you maintain an
   effective relationship.
2. Use the *Communication Styles Diagnostic Tool* to determine his or her preferred
   communication style.
3. Read through the *Matching Communication Styles* section below.
4. Now, make a list of three or four things you need to do more of in order to
   improve your communication effectiveness with this person.
5. Make a list of three or four things you need to do less of in order to improve your
   communication effectiveness with this person.

Communication Styles Diagnostic Tool

Low Assertive	High Assertive
❏ Waits to be introduced. ❏ Shakes hands gently. ❏ Makes intermittent eye contact. ❏ Speaks infrequently at meetings. ❏ Expresses opinions when asked. ❏ Good listener, more tentative. ❏ Makes decisions and changes slowly and cautiously. ❏ Asks clarifying questions. ❏ Risk-averse. If communicators are Low Assertive, then their Communication Style is either *Collaborative* or *Conscientious*.	❏ Introduces him- or herself. ❏ Shakes hands firmly. ❏ Makes sustained eye contact. ❏ Speaks frequently at meetings. ❏ Expresses opinions readily. ❏ Fast talker, persuasive presenter. ❏ Makes decisions and changes quickly or spontaneously. ❏ Asks rhetorical questions. ❏ Risk-taker. If communicators are High Assertive, then their Communication Style is either *Creative* or *Competitive*.
Low Expressive	**High Expressive**
❏ Task-oriented. ❏ Prefers to work independently. ❏ Appears reserved and somewhat formal. ❏ Guarded, and more difficult to get to know. ❏ Focuses on facts and issues. ❏ Makes decisions based on evidence and data. ❏ Pragmatic, realist. ❏ Self-contained, controlled. If communicators are Low Expressive, then their Communication Style is either *Conscientious* or *Competitive*.	❏ People-oriented. ❏ Prefers to work with others. ❏ Appears relaxed, warm, and friendly. ❏ Open, animated, and easy to get to know. ❏ Uses stories and anecdotes. ❏ Makes decisions based on feelings and values. ❏ Visionary, idealist. ❏ Passionate, enthusiastic. If communicators are High Expressive, then their Communication Style is either *Collaborative* or *Creative*

MATCHING COMMUNICATION STYLES

Competitive-Style

Competitive-Style communicators are assertive and reasonable, dominating, efficient, effective; lack patience; and need to be in control. Competitive-style communicators can be difficult to work with because in the extreme they can fall into the "It's my way or the highway" syndrome. They can believe they are always right, and much of the time they are. They are often insensitive to how their decisions and actions affect other people. In response to feedback, competitive-style communicators will often ignore you, blame others, express anger or resentment, and go on the attack.

Tips for dealing with a competitive style:

- Get to the point.
- Focus on results, the bottom line.
- Be prepared, well organized, logical, and concise.
- Don't take up too much of their time.
- Don't tell them what they should do.
- Offer options.
- You could earn their respect by challenging them, but only if you are skilled enough to compete at their level.
- Align your recommendations with their vision.
- Gain their trust by producing results in your area of responsibility.

Creative-Style

communicators are assertive and emotional, persuasive influencers who want attention, enjoy their freedom, are playful, and prefer finding new ways to do things. Creative-style communicators can be difficult to work with because in the extreme they can fall into the "It's all about me" syndrome. They can be very egotistical, and in need of constant attention. Being emotional and throwing a temper tantrum would not be out of character. People who are creative-style communicators are not good at staying on topic, or on following through on commitments.

Tips for dealing with a creative style:

- Get to know them personally away from work.
- Meet with them face-to-face.
- Allow an adequate amount of time for them to think out loud.
- Make it easy.
- Provide creative and innovative solutions, big ideas.
- Avoid too many details, facts, and figures.
- Offer immediate incentives.
- Engage them as active participants in a way that will be fun for them.
- Don't expect them to be very organized.
- Gain their trust by acknowledging how talented they are.
- Follow up with a brief summary of the decisions that were made and the next steps.

Collaborative-Style

communicators are receptive and emotional, supportive, agreeable, sociable; need to be involved; and need to trust you. Collaborative-style communicators can be difficult to work with because in the extreme they can fall into the "victim" or "martyr" syndrome. Often they will not be direct or candid about how they feel because they are afraid of hurting someone else's feelings. People who are collaborative-style communicators are often afraid of personal rejection, and may take constructive feedback as a statement about who they are rather than about their job performance.

Tips for dealing with a collaborative style:

- Build a personal relationship with them.
- Be supportive.
- Be available to them.

- Respond to their requests for your input.
- Involve them in your projects.
- Demonstrate personal commitment.
- Communicate with them one-on-one.
- Share with them how you *feel* when they are being difficult.
- Enlist their support in coming up with solutions for how you can work together more effectively.
- Gain their trust by showing concern for their well-being.

Conscientious-Style

communicators are receptive and reasonable, analytical thinkers who value accuracy, need things to be right and correct, and need closure and control. Conscientious-style communicators can be difficult to work with because in the extreme they can fall into the "gotcha syndrome" where they find an error to prove your incompetence. Their need to be precise in communications can cause others to feel they are talking down to them. Conscientious-style communicators can become rigid and stubborn if they think things are not being done in the right way. Since their greatest fear is to be wrong, conscientious-style communicators are likely to become defensive when being given feedback. They will typically respond by denying the problem and using data to prove their point.

Tips for dealing with a conscientious style:

- Be prepared.
- Provide information in writing.
- Pay attention to details.
- Provide specific facts and figures.
- Have a logical, step-by-step plan for improving the situation.
- Provide research-based documentation.
- Proofread everything carefully.
- Double-check all your facts.
- Gain their trust by following procedures and doing things by the book.
- Never surprise them.

6. Building a Communicating Community

To effectively communicate, we must realize that we are all different in the way we perceive the world and use this understanding as a guide to our communications with others.

—ANTHONY ROBBINS

PURPOSE

Now that you have the four communication styles as a model for appreciating different ways that individuals prefer to present and process information, you can apply these insights to improve how the group can work together more effectively as a team.

PROCEDURE

1. Divide into small groups and have each team member share his or her communication style. Record the communication style of each team member on a chart. As a group, discuss the implications of the team's communication styles and how this information explains some of the team's strengths as well as some of its challenges.
2. Have each team member share how he or she prefers to receive feedback, indicating how this is in keeping with his or her communication style. Give an example of when someone gave you feedback in a way that really worked for you. Create a set of guidelines for giving feedback to each of the communication styles that the team can use for future reference. See Table 2.2 for a synopsis of guidelines for giving feedback.
3. As a group, explore how communication styles influence decision-making behavior.
4. Have each person discuss specific examples of how he or she prefers to make decisions given his or her communication style. As a group, identify guidelines for working most effectively as a team that balance healthy relationships and impressive results.
5. Discuss the connections between communication styles and learning styles, and create a template that can be used by teachers when creating lesson plans.

TABLE 2.2 Sample Guidelines for Giving Feedback

General guidelines

Conscientious	Respect their competence, and be prepared with a specific request.
Creative	Respect their talent, and engage them in creating possible solutions.
Competitive	Respect their desire to take action, and get to the point.
Collaborative	Respect their commitment to contribute to you and the team, and enlist their help.

When giving positive feedback

Conscientious	Describe what they did that worked.
Creative	Acknowledge what was special about how they did it.
Competitive	Focus on what results were accomplished.
Collaborative	Share what personal attribute made a difference.

When giving constructive feedback on how to improve

Conscientious	State specifically what they could do to build on what they know.
Creative	Describe how they could make it even more exciting, and emphasize an immediate payoff.
Competitive	Focus on how greater results could be produced more efficiently.
Collaborative	Share how they could make it even more meaningful for others.

When discussing what they will do to act on the feedback

Conscientious	Focus on the next step in the process.
Creative	Invite them to come up with options.
Competitive	Ask them to decide from a set of options.
Collaborative	Let them know you are available to support them.

Speaking of giving feedback, here is a Zen story whose author is unknown.

36 YEARS OF SILENCE

An aspiring Monk wanted to find a Guru. He went to a monastery and his preceptor told him: "You can stay here but we have one important rule—all students observe the vow of silence. You will be allowed to speak in 12 years time."

After practicing for 12 long years silent meditation etc., the day came when the student could say his one thing or ask his one question. He said: "The bed is too hard."

He kept going for another 12 years of hard silent meditation and got the opportunity to speak again. He said: "The food is not good."

Twelve more years of hard work and he got to speak again. Here are his words after 36 years of practice: "I quit."

His Guru quickly answered: "Good, all you have been doing anyway is complaining."

In Conclusion

The main point to remember from this part of the book is that effective leadership cannot occur without effective communication.

- Absolute accuracy in communication is difficult. Even in the best of circumstances, communication is more an approximation than a certainty. The more context you provide, the greater the odds that what you truly said was correctly heard.
- Listening is not the same as waiting to talk.
- The real meaning of your communication is the result it produces.
- Your communication will resonate most clearly and persuasively when you deliver it in a manner that respects the other person's context and style.

PART THREE

TO LEAD IS TO ALIGN— COLLABORATION SKILLS

9 Strategies to Facilitate Collaboration

Legend has it that in the year 711 A.D. the commander of the Muslim army in Africa sent his slave, Tariq bin Ziyad, to Spain with a small group of Activists. When Tariq reached Spain and observed the enemy from every angle, he understood that they were bent upon attacking the Muslims.

Tariq ordered his men to burn down the ships in which they had reached the coast of Spain. When the ships began to burn, some took exception to that act and cried out, "Why are you doing this, Sir? How will we return to our homeland?"

"We have not come here to return," replied Tariq. "We have the enemy in front of us and the deep sea behind us. We shall now either defeat the enemy and win, or die a coward's death by drowning in the sea. Who will follow me?"

This forceful speech inspired much courage in the Muslim warriors. Tariq and his soldiers fought fearlessly, routed one of the most formidable armies of the West, and succeeded in conquering Spain.

"How," you might ask, "did they accomplish this?" The answer is total commitment to moving forward because going back was no longer an option.

—ISLAMIC LEGEND

My client—the president of a multinational media company—who recounted a version of this story went on to tell his team of managers that, like Tariq and his men, there was no turning back for them either. The organization was going through significant restructuring; the decisions had been made, the "ships had been burned," and everyone needed to get behind the changes that were planned.

I was there facilitating this management retreat, and while I do not believe in forcing alignment by eliminating all other options, having the president of the company announce that he was totally committed to following through on a path forward helped dissipate much of the resistance to change that would have, otherwise, dominated the conversation.

This section takes a collaborative approach to achieving alignment among members of the school community. Finding the right balance between asserting one's own ideas while being respectful of the ideas of others is an essential skill that underlies all of the lessons outlined here. You will learn when it is best for you to be the "decider" and when to seek group consensus. Team tools for finding innovative solutions to problems that concern your staff are laid out with step-by-step instructions for ease of use. It is my belief that when you engage hearts and minds, commitment will follow.

1. Facilitating "Learningful" Dialogue

When nothing is sure,
everything is possible.

—Margaret Drabble

PURPOSE

Someone calculated that the average child asks 300 questions a day, while the average adult asks six. This suggests that children are in "inquiry" mode much more often than adults.

Part Three of this book is designed to enhance your ability to create alignment, which is done by building connections of commonality between your needs and those of others, between your motivations and those of others, between your vision and those of others. The route to discovering these common connections is by balancing *inquiry*—discovering what others think and feel—with *advocacy*—telling others what you think and feel. The material in this lesson draws on the work of Peter Senge, Rick Ross, and Charlotte Roberts.[1] In his highly influential book *The Fifth Discipline*, Senge describes, " 'Learningful' conversations that balance inquiry and advocacy, where people expose their own thinking effectively and make that thinking open to the influence of others."

Sometimes it's appropriate for you, as a leader, to first establish your point of view and then invite others to react to your proposal. Other times it is more effective to start by inviting others to express their viewpoints before you formulate and communicate your decision. Whether you are more comfortable *asking* or *telling* will have a lot to do with your communication style (discussed in Part Two). Inquiry will seem more natural for collaborative and conscientious-style communicators, while competitive and creative-style communicators are more assertive in advocating for their viewpoint.

The general rule of thumb is this: Inquiry precedes advocacy.[2] In order to determine the best approach in a given situation, ask yourself these questions:

1. Am I confident that the information I have is reliable and complete?
2. Have I engaged and obtained input from all the relevant stakeholders?
3. Have I articulated a clear plan for implementing a realistic goal, and do I have sufficient support/power to put my plan into action?

If the answer to these three questions is yes, then it makes sense to go ahead and advocate your position, and align everyone behind you.

However, if you are uncertain about the quality of your information, have not yet involved the key stakeholders, and don't know the amount of support for your plan, then it would be wise for you to engage in further inquiry.

Inquiry involves talking with other people and learning from them. At this stage, you are not judging, arguing, or trying to present your own point of view. You are focused on really listening to and seeking to understand their context. You are also gathering relevant data so that you can make informed decisions.

Given that the purpose of the inquiry is to arrive at a joint understanding of how best to accomplish a goal or solve a problem, then it is appropriate to expand beyond just listening to openly exploring one another's perspectives and appreciating what experiences and assumptions led to others' conclusions. The guidelines for Dedicated Listening apply.

Advocacy usually involves "selling" an idea or a position, making a point, or taking a stand in an attempt to influence others. It typically includes supporting your viewpoint with a rational argument, or directing attention to certain facts you believe are relevant.

Advocacy is about how ideas are presented and explained. If you have not met the above-mentioned criteria of having quality information based on input from stakeholders backed by sufficient support, then advocacy is likely to come across as being dictatorial. At best, this approach might gain you compliance, but not commitment. People support what they help create. Effective advocacy is a dialogue—a learningful conversation—that builds on what has been discovered by inquiring into relevant data and various perspectives to arrive at a shared understanding.

Inquiry and Advocacy in Action

When you're in inquiry mode, you are essentially seeking to discover:

1. What data is being used as the basis for the recommended action?
2. What assumptions are being made that are influencing how the data is interpreted?
3. What thought process led to the conclusions that are being drawn?
4. How does this fit into a larger context?

When inquiring, communicate in a tone that is inviting and nonthreatening. Use language that invites exploring, and avoid triggering defensiveness. Appropriate questions during the inquiry phase include:

1. "What data do you have for that?" "Can you give me an example of what you mean?"

2. "What assumptions are you making based on your observations?"
3. "Can you help me understand your thinking?" "How did you arrive at that conclusion?"
4. "How does this relate to the broader issue, or to the other concerns we've been discussing?"

Similarly, when you are in advocacy mode, you want to make explicit:

1. What data you are using as the basis for your recommended action
2. What assumptions you've made that are influencing your interpretation of the data
3. What thought process leads you to the conclusions that you are drawing
4. How this fits into your larger context

Appropriate statements to make when advocating for your position include:

1. "This is the data on which I am basing my decision." "Let me give you an example of what I mean."
2. "I assumed that this was true based on the evidence I had."
3. "I came to this conclusion because. . ."
4. "To put this into a broader context, the implications of this decision are. . ."

Balancing Inquiry and Advocacy to Achieve Alignment

Here are some additional guidelines to use when seeking to find the right balance of inquiry and advocacy that will lead to alignment behind a shared purpose, goal, or decision.

When inquiring:

- Explain how your questions help to clarify your concerns and assumptions. "I'm asking you about your assumptions here because. . ."
- Compare your assumptions to those of others.
- Test what they say by asking for broader contexts, or for examples. "How would your proposal affect . . .? " "Is this similar to . . .?" "Can you describe a typical example?"
- Check your understanding of what they have said. "Am I correct that you're saying . . .?"
- Listen for new understandings that may emerge. True inquiry is not about asking questions to coerce others to come around to your point of view.

When advocating:

- Listen, stay open, and invite others to provide alternative views. "Do you see it differently?"
- Encourage others to explore your thinking, assumptions, and data without becoming defensive. "What do you think about what I have just said? What can you add?"
- Publicly test your conclusions and assumptions.
- Reveal when you are not completely clear, and invite others to add value, or help influence your thinking. "This is an area where I could use your help."

- Avoid cutting off discussion too soon by using your leadership position to drive to a conclusion. This will short-circuit progress toward alignment.

Research shows a direct co-relationship between inquiry and advocacy in team performance.[3] First, teams were ranked in terms of performance, as measured by profit and loss statements, customer satisfaction surveys, and 360 reviews by superiors, peers, and subordinates to the teams. Then conversations among team members were observed. Interactions were coded as "inquiry" if they involved a question aimed at exploring and examining a position, and as "advocacy" if they involved arguing in favor of the speaker's viewpoint.

The results indicted that high-performing teams were equally balanced—50% of the interactions were inquiry and 50% were advocacy. On the other hand, medium-performing teams were more weighted toward advocacy by a 2-to-1 ratio, and low-performing teams were more advocacy-oriented by a ratio of 3 to 1.

In this activity, you will have the opportunity to practice balancing inquiry and advocacy, and measure the effects on your team performance.

PROCEDURE

1. Divide into teams of six participants, and assume the role of a School Improvement Team that is meeting to take action on one of the agenda items provided on the *School Improvement Team Sample Agenda Items Worksheet*.
2. Each team selects a team leader and an observer. The team leader's role is to help the team select an agenda item and facilitate the team's discussion. The observer's job is to keep track of inquiry and advocacy behaviors on the part of the team leader, as well as of the team as a whole using the *Team Observer Worksheet* provided.
3. At the end of 15 minutes, the observer calls time to end the meeting.
4. The team discusses how productive it thought the meeting was, and rates the meeting process on a scale from 1 to 5: 1. Unproductive, 2. Somewhat productive, 3. Moderately productive, 4. Very productive, 5. Extremely productive.
5. The team discusses how comfortable it felt in expressing its opinions, and rates the meeting environment on a scale from 1 to 5: 1. Uncomfortable, 2. Somewhat comfortable, 3. Moderately comfortable, 4. Very comfortable, 5. Extremely comfortable.
6. The observer then reports to the team the percentage of inquiry behaviors compared to advocacy behaviors that he or she observed on the part of the team leader, and of the team as a whole, as noted on the *Team Observer Worksheet*.
7. The team reflects on the relationship between its assessments of productivity and comfort relative to the ratio of inquiry/advocacy behaviors.
8. The full group reconvenes to hear reports from each of the small groups. Productivity ratings are compared with inquiry/advocacy percentages to see if there is any co-relationship. The same is done with comfort ratings. The full group summarizes lessons learned and implications for future meetings.

School Improvement Team Sample Agenda Items Worksheet

Start Time _____

Choose one of the following agenda items to discuss for the next 15 minutes:

1. Student Mentor Program

The school is establishing a Student Mentor Program that is intended to benefit both the older students who will be serving as the mentors as well as the younger students who will be receiving the help.

Possible questions for discussion:

- How will the mentors be selected? What criteria will be used? Is it necessary that they have a high grade-point average for all subjects, or is it enough that they excel in the area in which they will be mentoring?
- How will the mentees be chosen?
- Is the mentoring limited to academic areas or could it include nonacademic areas such as sports, the arts, leadership class, etc.?
- What training will the mentors need?
- What is the time commitment for the students?
- What is the incentive for the mentors? Will they receive extra credit?

2. Character Education Week

The school has scheduled a Character Education Week that will concentrate on Character Education, Civic Education, and Service Learning, including the seven traits of courage, integrity, kindness, perseverance, respect, responsibility, and self-discipline.

Possible questions for discussion:

- How would we like to see this structured?
- What are we really trying to accomplish? What are the instructional objectives of the activities that will be offered?
- What are the students expected to learn, and will they be graded?
- Is there a curriculum we are supposed to be following?
- Would the program be the focus of every class throughout the entire week or just some selected periods?
- Should Character Education be tied to the regular curriculum wherever possible?
- Will there be special assemblies during this week? If so, how would that time be used?
- Will we be organizing field trips during this week focused on relevant experiences?

At the end of the discussion, please rate the following items:

As a team, discuss how productive you thought the meeting was, and rate the meeting process on a scale from 1 to 5. *1. Unproductive, 2. Somewhat productive, 3. Moderately productive, 4. Very productive, 5. Extremely productive.*

Productivity Score _____

As a team, discuss how comfortable you felt in expressing your opinions, and rate the meeting environment on a scale from 1 to 5. *1. Uncomfortable, 2. Somewhat comfortable, 3. Moderately comfortable, 4. Very comfortable, 5. Extremely comfortable.*

Comfort Score_____

Team Observer Worksheet

While the team is meeting, observe its behavior and put a check mark in the appropriate box recording instances when the team leader as well as the team members are engaging in behavior that is consistent with inquiry and with advocacy. At the end of the meeting, tally up the totals to determine what percentage of time was spent in each of the modes.

INQUIRY	ADVOCACY
Examples:	Examples:
• Asking a question	• Making a statement
• Listening actively	• Selling an idea
• Encouraging further dialogue	• Taking a stand
• Open body language	• Commanding body language
• Restating to ensure accurate understanding	• Presenting a point of view
• Asking for supporting data	• Making a persuasive argument
• Testing assumptions	• Providing supportive data
• Exploring how conclusions were arrived at	• Asserting one's assumptions
	• Reiterating one's conclusions

Team Leader %	Team Leader %

Team Members %	Team Members %

2. Knowing *How* You Decide Can Be as Important as *What* You Decide

No, you don't make everybody happy, but if people feel they were listened to, they're going to be much more likely to go along with a decision.

—Drew Gilpin Faust

PURPOSE

Decisiveness is a trait we admire in a leader, but then so is inclusiveness. When is it better to just make the decision and get on with it? When is it better to involve others and try to reach consensus? Often, the approach to decision making is determined by the leader's personality. Each communication style, for example, has its strengths and blind spots when it comes to decision making. The following are some characteristic traits:

Conscientious: The bias is toward stability. Decisions have to make sense based on past experience. Asks, "What are the facts?" "How can we be sure it will work?" "What are the next steps?"

Creative: The bias is toward innovation. Decisions should creatively make use of new opportunities and insights. Asks, "What are the possibilities?" "How is this different from what we've done before?" "What would make it fun?"

Competitive: The bias is toward effectiveness. Decisions must be objective and logical. Asks, "How can we best achieve our goal?" "What's the point?" "Why are we wasting time talking about this?"

Collaborative: The bias is toward integrity. Decisions should consider people's values and needs. Asks, "How does this affect those involved?" "How does everyone feel about this?" "Wouldn't it be better to wait until all the members of the team are present before we decide?"

A more effective way of making the right decision in the right way is to adapt to the needs of the specific situation by considering three major factors: time, information, and commitment.

Time

If time is of the essence—you are in an emergency or crisis situation—it is faster to make a unilateral decision. If a fire broke out in one wing of the school, no one would expect you to call a staff meeting to discuss options and come to consensus on a course of action. They would expect you to act immediately to handle the situation.

In nonemergencies, when time is available to consult with others regarding a decision that will affect them, you would be wise to do so. While it would still be faster for you to just make the decision alone, you will probably discover yourself spending more time and effort dealing with questions and complaints, resentment and grousing, resistance and sometimes outright sabotage when you attempt to implement a decision in which others had no say.

Information

If you are an expert in the area and are confident that you know everything you need to in order to make the right decision, then it may be safe for you to do so. On the other hand, if you recognize that there are others whose depth of knowledge in certain areas is greater than yours, then adding their perspectives during the decision-making process would probably be smart.

Commitment

If the ultimate success of the decision you are making depends on the support and commitment of those who will be implementing it, then involving them during the decision-making process would be important.

Applying the three factors of time, information, and commitment, we can now consider which of seven different decision-making styles is most appropriate to a given situation.[4] As we progress from Style 1: Decide and Inform, to Style 7: Delegate, responsibility for the success of the decision moves from being yours alone to being more fully shared by the team.

Individual Decision Making

In individual decision making, the leader makes the decision alone and input from others is limited to collecting relevant information.

Style 1—You decide and inform others.

Style 2—You collect relevant information, decide, and inform.

Decision Making through Consultation

In consultation, the leader shares the issue with one or more people—seeking ideas, opinions, and suggestions—and then makes a decision. The leader considers the input of others, but the final decision may or may not be influenced by it. Style 4 is preferable to style 3 when there are apt to be strong differences of opinion, and it would be helpful if everyone could hear the different perspectives.

> *Style 3*—You consult with others individually seeking their ideas, opinions, and suggestions; then you decide.
>
> *Style 4*—You bring the group together to ask for its input, and then you make the decision.

Group Decision Making

In style 5, the leader wants the group to work together to resolve its differences and agree on a recommendation. In the case of style 6, the leader and others work together until they reach a consensus decision. Each group member's opinion and point of view are considered. As a result of helping to make the decision, group members buy into the final decision and commit to supporting its implementation.

> *Style 5*—You bring the group together and ask it to come up with a recommendation on which you can base your decision.
>
> *Style 6*—You and the group work together until you reach a consensus decision.

It is not always necessary or appropriate to use group decision making. If you have some doubt as to whether or not the group shares your goals, then you should be careful to not give up your decision-making authority. Teams that have worked together successfully for a while and have developed a high degree of trust with each other are more willing to support each other's decisions without always having to be involved. Another consideration when deciding to involve the group or not is whether the issue is of a confidential nature, which would preclude involving others in the decision.

Delegating the Decision

When delegating a decision, the leader sets the parameters and then allows one or more others to make the final decision. Although the leader does not make the decision, he or she supports it.

> *Style 7*—You delegate the decision to someone else or to the group.

PROCEDURE

1. Three *Decision-Making Scenarios* are presented below for your consideration. Use the *Decision-Making Worksheet* to help you determine which of the seven decision-making styles would be most appropriate in each situation. Give your rationale for that decision.
2. After you have completed your analysis of all three scenarios, get together in teams of three and use the *Decision-Making Styles* document to decide which decision-making style is being used in each of the three scenarios.

3. Share with each other the decision-making style you chose for each of the three scenarios along with your rationale.
4. In instances where the three of you came to different conclusions about which style was appropriate to the situation, use your skills of inquiry and advocacy to confirm the facts presented in the scenario, what assumptions were made by each of you, and how this resulted in different conclusions being drawn.

Decision-Making Scenarios

Scenario 1: Incentives Program

The School Improvement Team has come up with a proposal that the school create an incentives program to be used to motivate students. One of the ideas that has been discussed is soliciting local businesses to donate gift certificates that students could use to purchase merchandise in their stores. The certificates would be given to students at an awards night, and the business owners would be acknowledged publicly for their support.

The team has asked for your help in sending out a survey to all students, staff, and parents to determine what incentives would be most effective, and for what accomplishments and/or behaviors students should be rewarded. You need to decide whether or not to allow them to proceed with this idea.

You have three primary concerns. First, you're not certain how many students will actually respond to these incentives. High-performing students are already motivated. Students on the low end of the motivational spectrum probably won't care. So are there enough students in the middle for whom this would make a difference?

You are also worried that some staff and parents might object to the commercialization of education. Promoting retail stores at a school event might be considered crass. Would you need a policy about what types of business establishments could participate (i.e., Are candy stores OK? What about liquor stores? Tattoo parlors? etc.).

A third potential problem could arise with the superintendent. You happen to know that she is not likely to be a fan of this idea. She has on many occasions spoken about the value of intrinsic motivation. "Our mission," she would say, "is to create life-long learners who pursue knowledge for its own sake."

What decision-making style or sequence of styles would you use in this situation?

What is your rationale?

Scenario 2: Cutting Costs

Due to state budget cuts, your district office recently announced a mandatory 10% reduction in teacher supplements; those are the monies paid to staff for additional duties

Decision-Making Scenarios, *continued*

that include grade chairs, team leaders, morning and afternoon supervisions, lunch duty, honor society sponsors, and coaching responsibilities. At your school, this is a sizable amount of money—close to $50,000 each year.

You are not exactly sure how many teachers actually count on this additional income, and how many volunteer for more than one extra paid duty.

You need to decide which of these duties are essential to school operations, and which ones can be eliminated. Then you need to decide the fairest way of redistributing these duties to the teachers so as to minimize the impact on staff morale.

What decision-making style or sequence of styles would you use in this situation?

What is your rationale?

Scenario 3: Spending Money

Good news! You have just been informed that your school will receive $75,000 in state bonus money for posting successful results on your state mastery tests. This is wonderful recognition for your hardworking staff, and fortunately, the money comes with very few strings attached.

Now, the bad news. You need to decide how to spend the money, or how to involve the 75 people on your staff in deciding how to spend it.

You feel strongly that the staff deserves to share in the money. But who on the staff should receive bonuses, how much should they receive, and who gets to decide? You are guessing that everyone will have an opinion about "who works the most" or "who deserves it the most." One option would be to divide the money equally among all staff members—including custodians, teachers, cafeteria workers, aides, administrators, and front office staff.

In addition to trying to get agreement among the staff, you are also going to need the approval of the School Advisory Council (SAC). The SAC is made up of parents, teachers, local businesspeople, and community representatives from all of the cultures represented in your school. You can almost certainly count on the teachers to be in favor of staff bonuses, but you expect that others would argue that the money is better spent on equipment and supplies that the school needs.

What decision-making style or sequence of styles would you use in this situation?

What is your rationale?

Decision-Making Worksheet

Use the questions below as a guide to choosing a decision-making style.

	Yes	No	
1. *Do you have a reasonable amount of time to make the decision?*	☐	☐	If yes, consider styles 2, 3, 4, 5, 6, 7.
2. *Do you need more information to make a good decision?*	☐	☐	If yes, consider styles 2, 3, 4, 5, 6, 7.
3. *Do you want input and suggestions from others to help you make a good decision?*	☐	☐	If yes, consider styles 3, 4, 5, 6, 7.
4. *Is there an advantage to bringing the group together so that it can hear other perspectives?*	☐	☐	If yes, consider styles 4, 5, 6, 7.
5. *Is there likely to be conflict in the group, which members should be encouraged to resolve?*	☐	☐	If yes, consider styles 5, 6, 7.
6. *Is commitment to the decision by the group critical?*	☐	☐	If yes, consider style 6.
7. *Does the group have the expertise to make the decision itself, and do you trust that group members share your goals and will come up with a decision you can support?*	☐	☐	If yes, consider style 7.

Decision-Making Styles

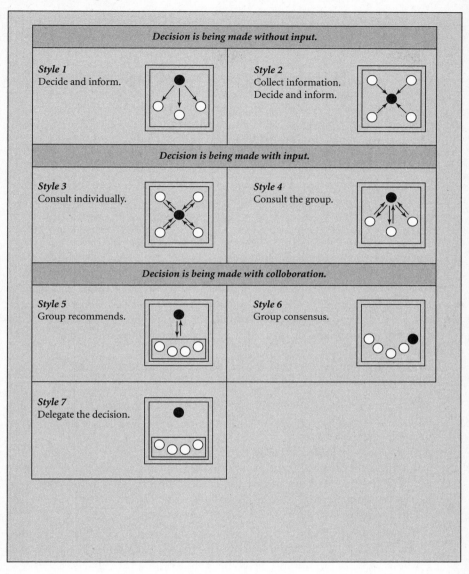

3. Building Consensus

Exchange is creation.

—MURIEL RUKEYSER

PURPOSE

Of the decision-making styles discussed in the last lesson, Style 6: Group Consensus, is the most difficult to employ successfully. Consensus is a decision-making process where the group agrees on a decision that all members can support. The degree of collaboration required to reach consensus distinguishes this method from other styles of group decision making.

In order to ensure success with consensus decision making, you need to provide for the following conditions:

- Sufficient time to present and discuss all the relevant information, opinions, and options; and to debate and resolve different proposals, objections, and obstacles to agreeing on a decision
- Strong facilitative leadership skills
- Willingness on the part of the group members to contribute their views honestly, and to be open to considering the views of others
- Recognition on the part of the group members that the *benefits* of their coming together to agree on a decision are worth the *costs*
  - Potential *benefits* include: everyone has the opportunity to influence the outcome, confidence that the process led to the best decision for the group as a whole, sense of community resulting from working through the issues to a successful conclusion.
  - Possible *costs* include: time invested in the process, potential discomfort of having to deal with disagreement and conflict, and having to give up any version of the "my-way-or-the-highway" approach to negotiating one's needs.

In general, the *advantages* of consensus decision making include:

- Greater sense of ownership for the decision, resulting in shared responsibility for its success

- Higher degree of commitment to supporting the successful implementation of the decision, resulting in greater willingness to find solutions rather than find fault when things don't go exactly according to plan.
- Enhanced creativity required to reach consensus likely to result in a higher-quality decision.
- Increased effectiveness of the learning community, resulting from applying the values of cooperation, mutual trust, community, and fairness.

The *disadvantages* include:

- Consensus is slow. Decisions can be made much more quickly in a hierarchy model where the person at the top is empowered to act, or in a committee that gets to decide based on which side has the most votes.
- Consensus can be frustrating. If the process doesn't result in consensus support for any specific course of action, the group may feel ineffectual and demoralized.
- Consensus is not always possible. As groups get large, consensus becomes more difficult. Unlike voting, where the majority can decide to act against the objections of those in the minority, consensus requires a common purpose and shared goals in order for decisions to be made. If people have fundamentally different desires, consensus may be impossible.

Consensus doesn't mean that everyone is totally satisfied with the group's ultimate decision. Obviously, it's not possible for everyone to get his or her first choice. It does mean that everyone can say:

- I had the opportunity to communicate my views and opinions.
- I believe that the other members of the group actively listened to me, and gave consideration to my ideas.
- I actively listened to and considered the ideas and views of the other group members.
- I believe that we used a process that was fair, and that led us to the decision on what's best for us as a group.
- I agree to support this decision and work toward its successful implementation.

If consensus cannot be achieved, or at least can't be achieved within an agreed upon period of time, then it should be made clear what alternative style would be used to make the decision. For example, you could use style 5, which would involve asking the group to come up with its best recommendation on which you can base your decision. The recommendation could be arrived at through voting, and minority points of view could be spelled out so that everyone's opinions are clear before you decide. Another option is Style 4, which essentially means that you take the material generated during the meeting and use it as input as you ultimately make the decision.

It's worth noting that *group consensus* is not *groupthink*. Groupthink is a defective decision-making process that can arise when members confuse congeniality with consensus, and seek harmony over clarity.

A well-documented example of groupthink used by many group studies is the Bay of Pigs fiasco. The group of advisors surrounding President John F. Kennedy apparently was so intent on showing unanimity in their support for the president's goal to overthrow Castro that they could not, or would not, see the readily available information clearly indicating that the invasion would fail miserably. Solidarity became the driving force over sound judgment.

After the Bay of Pigs incident, JFK—learning from his mistakes—sought to avoid groupthink during the Cuban Missile Crisis. He was deliberately absent from some of the meetings so as to avoid pressing his own opinion. Outside experts were invited to share their viewpoints, and group members were allowed to question them carefully.

Also, to break group cohesion, subgroups were formed and various departments met separately to discuss possible solutions. Thanks in part to these measures, the missile crisis was ultimately resolved peacefully.

To avoid making the kinds of bad decisions that can result from groupthink, consider JFK's example.

- Let the group meet without you for at least part of the time.
- Avoid over-influencing the group by trying to lead them toward your preferred solution.
- Encourage everyone to voice his or her objections and doubts.
- Assign the group into subgroups and ask each to evaluate the problem.
- Invite outside experts to challenge the group's decision.
- Insist that everyone apply Dedicated Listening guidelines.
- Facilitate a balance between inquiry and advocacy behaviors.
- Create a set of Team Agreements that can be used consistently to govern group behavior.

The purpose of this lesson is to practice one method that can be used in gaining group consensus. It has the added benefit of resulting in a set of agreements designed to enhance team relationships and improve team results.

PROCEDURE

Achieving Consensus on Team Agreements

1. Define *Team Agreements*. For example, "Team Agreements are a set of commitments we will make as a group about how we want to treat each other, and how we want to work together." Read the sample Team Agreements provided.
2. Develop a set of Team Agreements you would like to see the group adopt.
3. Pair up and integrate two separate lists into one set of Team Agreements that you both support. Share your individual Team Agreements and identify those that are similar that you can easily combine. Discuss any agreements that were on one person's list but not the other's to determine if you would like to include these in the final list. Any proposed Team Agreement that cannot be rewritten so both members of the pair can support it is omitted from the joint list.
4. Now, each pair gets together with another pair to form a team of four. They, in turn, share the list from each of the pairs, and integrate them into one list the four of you can support.
5. Continue this process—teams of four become teams of eight, etc.—until you end up with two final lists. Depending on the total number of people in your

group, you may need to make some adjustments. For example, if you start off with an odd number, you could have teams of three people working together.

6. As a full group, discuss the final two sets of Team Agreements. Combine into one final list that everyone agrees to support.

7. This exercise can be turned into a Team Contract by leaving space for participants to sign their names and signify their commitment to keeping these agreements. The Team Agreements can also be posted in the staff room or classroom. See the *Sample Team Agreements* document for examples.

Sample Team Agreements

- I agree to communicate with clarity and respect, always keeping my intentions transparent.
- I agree to listen to others and respect their points of view.
- I agree to give others the benefit of the doubt, and to assume that they, too, are operating with the best interests of the school community at heart.
- I agree to respect and honor the expertise of my co-workers.
- When I have a problem with someone, I agree to address it directly with that person openly and honestly in the spirit of partnership.
- I agree to provide honest, constructive feedback in a positive manner to fellow staff members.
- I agree to accept constructive feedback respectfully and graciously.
- I agree to take responsibility for my own actions, including my mistakes.
- I agree to come to meetings on time and prepared.
- I agree to involve other staff members in decisions that will affect them, and to be respectful of their workload when making requests for their time.

4. Solving Problems Collaboratively

*Too many problem-solving sessions become
battlegrounds where decisions are made based on power
rather than intelligence.*

—Margaret J. Wheatley

PURPOSE

As was discussed earlier, there are some decisions that are best made by group consensus. When a high degree of commitment is required to ensure the successful implementation of a solution to a problem that affects a large portion of the school community, then it is wise to use a collaborative style that encourages the full participation of all the stakeholders.

The next four activities provide a logical sequence for tackling a problem in a collaborative manner. There are many different problem-solving models, most of which have the same elements:

Phase 1—Identify the problem.

Phase 2—Generate alternative solutions.

Phase 3—Decide on the best solution.

Phase 4—Develop an implementation plan.

We will be using the terms "Inquisitor," "Designer," "Evaluator," and "Activist" (I.D.E.A.) as analogies for the four phases in the process because each suggests a certain mindset about how to approach each particular phase.

The first phase in the process, **Inquisitor**, seeks to define the "real" problem so that any solutions that are implemented actually accomplish what's needed. Often solutions address the symptoms of a problem rather than the root causes.

Once the problem is defined, the next phase, **Designer**, invites you to put your creative thinking caps on to generate as many potential solutions as possible.

Next, **Evaluator** is the phase where the potential solutions are evaluated in order to determine which one is likely to be most effective in solving the problem.

Finally, **Activist** is when you develop a plan outlining the actions needed to implement the solution.

The process is meant to be highly interactive, building group consensus on the problem definition as well as on the final solution. Strong facilitation is critical. Each phase in the process must remain distinct, be taken in sequence and completed before proceeding with the process.

The group needs to agree that it has accurately defined the problem before moving on to solving it. Likewise, judgment needs to be deferred until after brainstorming since nothing puts a damper on creative thinking more than having a critic in the group negating some of the suggestions.

PROCEDURE

1. The team leader posts four large pieces of poster or easel paper on one wall so that they are visible to all the participants, and prints one of these words on the top of each page in this order: INQUISITOR, DESIGNER, EVALUATOR, ACTIVIST.
2. Starting with INQUISITOR, the group brainstorms attitudes and behaviors consistent with the idea of being an Inquisitor. (Typical answers include: curious, inquisitive, open-minded, asks questions, probes beneath the surface, etc.)
3. After everyone feels the discussion regarding Inquisitor is complete, the group moves on to DESIGNER by asking what attitudes and behaviors are consistent with the idea of being a Designer. (Typical answers include: creative, visionary, different way of seeing things, unconventional, etc.)
4. Once again, when the group is done with Designer, focus on the EVALUATOR by asking what attitudes and behaviors are consistent with the idea of being an Evaluator. (Typical answers include: decisive, fair, objective, fact-based, etc.)
5. Final phase is the ACTIVIST. (Typical answers include: committed, passionate, driven, courageous, etc.)
6. Locate the *Collaborative Problem-Solving Overview* and discuss how this model might be an effective tool for solving school-related problems. Brainstorm what types of problems would or would not be appropriate for applying this four-phase process.
7. Now choose one school-related problem you will analyze using the four collaborative problem-solving steps outlined in the next four activities. Consider applying the following criteria to selecting the most appropriate problem on which to focus your efforts:

    • Important enough to warrant the investment of time and energy.
    • Time is available to allow for adequate consideration.
    • Collaboration is critical to successful implementation.
    • People who are most affected are in a position to solve it.

Collaborative Problem-Solving Overview

INQUISITOR
- Examine all major aspects of the problem.
- Build understanding on the core issues.
- Agree on the real problem.
- State the problem in the form of a question.

DESIGNER
- Brainstorm possible solutions.
- Invite creative ideas.
- Avoid extensive discussions.
- Defer judgment.
- Have fun.

EVALUATOR
- Reduce the total number of options.
- Combine similar items.
- Establish selection criteria.
- Eliminate ideas that are not feasible.
- Rank the remaining ideas.
- Discuss pros and cons.
- Achieve consensus on the best solution(s).

ACTIVIST
- Develop an Action Plan that includes:
  - Specific steps.
  - Timeline.
  - Persons responsible.
  - Resources required.
  - Mechanism for monitoring progress.

5. Transforming Problems Into Opportunities

A problem well stated is a problem half solved.

—CHARLES F. KETTERING

PURPOSE

Problem identification is undoubtedly the most important? and the most difficult phase of the process. How a problem is stated determines the type and quality of solutions that are identified. So, framing the problem in the most effective way is a critical phase in the process.

By definition, the existence of a problem indicates that the current situation is not the ideal situation. Defining where you are now (situation analysis) relative to where you want to be (goal identification) is a good way to start exploring the problem.

Problems don't exist in a vacuum. They exist in a larger context and are influenced by factors that should be taken into account before trying to create possible solutions. If you don't correctly identify the real problem, you are likely to end up treating the symptoms rather than correcting the true cause of the problem.

The purpose of this lesson is to increase the team's ability to solve problems effectively by learning to first define and diagnose them accurately. You probably need more than one meeting to complete the steps outlined in this procedure.

PROCEDURE

1. Remind yourself what it means to be an "Inquisitor." Seeking to discover what's going on by asking questions, gathering data, and analyzing the facts are all appropriate ways of approaching this part of the process. On the other hand, suggesting ways to solve the problem, evaluating what might work, or describing actions that could be taken are all behaviors that are not appropriate here, and should be saved for later.

2. The purpose of this lesson is for the group to reach agreement on a definition of the real problem. The intended result is to transform the problem into an opportunity by framing it as a question that will lead to an innovative solution and effective action.

3. In the last lesson, you identified a school-related problem to use for this series of exercises. Start the dialogue by asking, "How would I define the problem?" The team leader will record all team members' answers on a flip chart, white board, or on sticky notes. As an example, let's work on the problem of teachers and related services staff not having enough collaborative planning time.

4. Now ask, "What is the current situation?" or "Where are we now relative to this problem?" Alternative versions include: "How problematic is it?" "How serious is the situation?" "What does the data indicate is true about current performance?"
   A description of the current situation might be, for example,

   The only scheduled time for teams to meet is during a 20-minute working lunch, which only happens once a week.

5. The next step is to consider the desired future situation once the problem has been addressed. Ask, "Where do we want to be with regard to this situation?" Alternative questions include: "What level of success do we imagine is possible?" "What is our goal in this area?"
   It might be determined, for example,

   Teams need to meet at least three times per week for an hour at a time.

6. Now, write a statement of the problem that contrasts the current situation with your desired goal by combining the answers to the questions asked in Steps 4 and 5.
   For example,

   The problem is that teachers and related services staff only have time to meet for 20 minutes per week, when they need to meet for three hours per week to do collaborative planning.

7. Next, the group explores the context in which this problem exists by creating a mind map. The team leader can post a large sheet of paper on the wall so that all members of the group can see it. In the center of the page, print what the problem is that you are exploring. The group then brainstorms the relevant factors that influence this problem. Record each relevant factor that is mentioned by putting keywords or images on the map using different-colored markers. Some of the factors may be closely related, which can be represented by placing them near each other on the map. Other elements associated with the main ideas may be connected like branches on a tree.
   Some key questions include:

   • What are the relevant factors that are contributing to this problem?
   • Which factors are related to structure (i.e., school culture, policies, scheduling, decision-making authority, etc.)?
   • Which factors are related to process (planning, training, managing, etc.)?
   • Which factors are related to people (lack of support, lack of communication, lack of flexibility, etc.)?

Other questions you can ask to reveal more of the context include:

- What are the parameters of the problem? What is or is not part of the problem?
- Where is the problem? In what situations does the problem arise?
- When is it a problem?
- What makes it a problem?
- Whose problem is it? Who owns it? Who is most affected by it?
- Is this a new problem or a recurring problem?

Continue this process until everyone has a good sense of how the problem fits within a larger context.

8. The next step is to take a fresh look at all that has been identified as part of the context of the problem and distinguish between what aspects are based on factual evidence, and what aspects are based on assumptions, interpretations, or beliefs. One way of doing this is to use a colored marker to circle the items that everyone agrees are facts.

9. Now the group can summarize its understanding of the problem by answering these three questions:

- What do we agree that we know about the problem?
- What do we agree we don't we know?
- What else do we need to know in order to consider possible solutions?

If there are things that still need to be known about the problem, then you need an action plan for gathering the data needed to finish defining the problem before moving on to identifying possible solutions. Make a list of what information needs to be collected and disseminated to the group.

Determine if the data already exists and, if so, where. If new research needs to be conducted, decide on how this will be done. Establish who is going to be responsible for which action steps, and agree on a timeline for completing these tasks.

10. The final step in completing the Inquisitor phase is to frame the problem as an opportunity by writing it as an actionable question, which can then be used during the Designer phase as the basis for generating possible solutions. Write the following sentence structure on easel pages so that the group can work on this together:

- *How can . . . (subject) . . . (action verb) . . . (object). . . so that . . . (intended result)?*
- Decide who is the subject of the sentence (i.e., those individuals or groups empowered to solve the problem).

For example,

How can we (administrators and staff). . .?

- To determine which verb is appropriate, consider whether the subject has direct or indirect control over solving the problem. Verbs indicating direct control include: *act, develop, create, change, transform, reform, restructure,* etc. Verbs indicating indirect control include: *influence, inform, communicate, educate, persuade, motivate,* etc.

For example,

How can we (administrators and staff) restructure . . .?

- The object could be people (e.g., person responsible, person with resources, stakeholders, etc.), process (e.g., planning, training, performance management, etc.), or structure (e.g., school culture, policies, decision-making authority, etc.).

    For example,

    How can we (administrators and staff) restructure the schedule. . .?

- Finally, the intended result should refer to the desired goal identified in step 5.

    For example,

    How can we (administrators and staff) restructure the schedule so that teachers and related services staff can meet at least three times per week for an hour at a time for collaborative planning?

6. Creating Innovative Solutions

*Creativity is inventing, experimenting, growing, taking
risks, breaking rules, making mistakes, and having fun.*

—MARY LOU COOK

PURPOSE

Having completed the Inquisitor phase of the four-phase process, it is now time for
phase 2, Designer. The purpose is to generate as many solutions as possible to the
problem/question being considered.

PROCEDURE

1. The team leader sets up the room by posting easel pages on the wall so that
   group members can see the ideas as they are recorded. A volunteer takes notes on
   the pages.
2. Review what it means to be a Designer—creative, innovative, visionary, unconventional, etc. The purpose of this session is to brainstorm as many potential
   solutions as possible and to avoid editing thoughts or prejudging any ideas.
3. The team leader or volunteer writes the problem/question identified during the
   Inquisitor step on a chart and posts it so that everyone can see it. (Refer back to
   this problem/question throughout the process.)
       In our example:

   *How can we (administrators and staff) restructure the schedule so that
   teachers and related services staff can meet at least three times per week for
   an hour at a time for collaborative planning?*

4. As a group, review guidelines for brainstorming:
   - Everyone contributes as many ideas as possible.
   - Okay to piggyback on others' ideas.
   - Avoid discussing ideas at this point.
   - Defer judgment until the next phase.

5. As a group, establish an objective and time limit. For example, "Let's see if we can generate 20 ideas in the next 15 minutes." As each person shares an idea, the team leader can repeat it to make sure that everyone heard it, and to support the recorder in writing it accurately. Some examples of possible solutions to the problem of finding collaborative planning time identified by other schools[5] include:

   - *Use substitute teachers on a rotating basis to free grade-level teachers to plan together monthly or quarterly.*
   - *Schedule special area subject teachers (physical education, computer technology, art, music) at the same time in the same grade level to allow grade-level team members to meet together.*
   - *Identify the teachers who may need one or two occasions for extra time together to address a specific issue or concern. These teachers may be given a duty-free time block, coverage for early morning arrival, or end of day dismissal time.*
   - *The school principal or assistant principal provides periodic coverage of classes when the classroom teacher needs to meet with related service providers.*
   - *One teacher dismisses two classes so that the other teacher can plan with related service providers.*
   - *Once a month, the time designated for faculty meetings is used for grade-level collaboration between general educators and resource teachers.*
   - *When classes are combined for assemblies or to free a teacher for collaborative planning, parent volunteers provide students with additional encouragement and supervision so teachers can meet together.*
   - *Schedule teams to have the same lunch periods immediately followed by a common preparation period.*
   - *Develop a course for professional development credit that is structured to document teacher time and products. Teachers who sign up for the course meet after school, often with a school system consulting teacher, to design innovative plans for students with intense needs, and to plan to implement accommodations and modifications for an upcoming unit.*

6. If the ideas begin to wane before enough possible solutions have been proposed, look at the problem/question from different perspectives. For example,

   - "If you were in charge, how would you solve it?"
   - "If you were an outside consultant known for innovative solutions, what would you recommend?"
   - "If you were starting a school from scratch, and could organize it so that this problem didn't exist, what would you do?"

7. If some people have not offered any ideas, switch to a "round-robin" style where instead of group members calling out ideas at random, members can share their ideas one at a time, in rotation.

8. At the end of the brainstorming session, the team leader summarizes the results. Before moving on to the next phase, restate the problem/question and acknowledge the group's creativity in generating all these possible solutions.

9. If the group is not satisfied with the number of quality ideas on the brainstormed list, give yourselves more time by creating an "incubation period." Collect more

ideas after a break or a few days later. Each person can record ideas on a 3 × 5 pad of sticky notes. A fun suggestion is to also provide a small penlight for group members to keep on their bedside night table so that if they have any brainstorms in the middle of the night, they can record them before such ideas are forgotten.

SUPPLEMENTARY MATERIAL: ADDITIONAL "DESIGNER" TOOLS

VARIATIONS ON TRADITIONAL BRAINSTORMING

Brainstorming With Sticky Notes

PURPOSE

This technique speeds the collecting, sorting, and reorganizing of ideas by about three times over traditional brainstorming where a facilitator or recorder/scribe writes ideas on flip charts.

PROCEDURE

1. Each participant will need a 3 × 5 pad of sticky notes along with a dark felt-tip pen.
2. Groups can be made up of teams of approximately six to eight participants.
3. Instructions on how to use the sticky notes:
   - Write down one idea per note.
   - Write large so everyone can read it.
   - Write at least five words per idea, including a noun and a verb.
   - Record longer ideas by sticking multiple notes together.
4. The goal of this activity is to create as many innovative solutions as possible to solve the problem identified during the Inquisitor phase. The problem/question can be written on the white board or flip chart where the sticky notes will be posted.
5. Next, everyone can work on their own in silence to write three to six ideas on sticky notes.
6. Participants stand in a circle around the white board or flip chart so that they can share their ideas by posting the notes where everyone on their team can see them. Each person reads his or her ideas out loud as they are posted. As with traditional brainstorming, all ideas are good ideas, and no judging is allowed.
7. After everyone has read out loud and posted all of the sticky notes they generated individually, participants can add any additional ideas they thought of while listening to their teammates.
8. When the brainstorming phase is over, each participant selects one idea from all of those generated that he or she thinks would be most effective in solving the problem. As these priority ideas are selected, move the corresponding sticky note to the top of the white board or flip chart.
9. Participants can group subideas under each main idea.
10. Reflection and summarizing statements from the group can be elicited before concluding this activity.
11. Now it is time for the "Evaluator" to take over and have the group come to consensus on which of these big ideas should be implemented.

A Straw Man Proposal

PURPOSE

A "blank slate" brainstorming session is not always the most efficient or effective way to create a solid solution to a problem. In some situations, you may get better and faster results by giving people something to which they can react. Enter the "Straw Man Proposal."

A straw man is a first draft or prototype used to invite feedback, criticism, and testing. It can be a good place to start the Designer phase of the collaborative problem-solving process by giving the team the inspiration it needs to think innovatively and gain momentum toward coming up with a solution.

A straw man proposal is useful in ensuring that everyone involved has a tangible concept from which to work. Otherwise, there is a risk that team members might be working with different perceptions and unstated assumptions as they discuss aspects of the idea or solution.

PROCEDURE

How you develop your straw man proposal depends on the situation and the resources available. A typical process would include:

1. Create a draft proposal or prototype based on your initial judgment and experience.
2. Present your draft proposal to the team and tell everyone that it is a straw man. (This is critical because all team members must clearly understand that your idea is the starting point, and was created for the purpose of knocking it down and rebuilding something much better.)
3. The group analyzes the proposal, finds its weak points, clarifies assumptions and decision-making criteria, and works on a refined proposal.

E-mail Brainstorming

E-mail can be used in conjunction with face-to-face meetings to help facilitate brainstorming and problem solving. For instance, if there are stakeholders who are not part of the core team that is working on solving the problem but have expertise or points of view that need to be considered, their input can be solicited via e-mail.

Also, in advance of a team brainstorming session, you could save time by e-mailing the problem statement to the attendees and asking them to submit their views of the problem and two or three possible solutions prior to the meeting. You could then organize a draft proposal to circulate to everyone that might include the three or four most commonly cited solutions to the problem. By putting possible solutions in front of the team members beforehand, more progress can be made when you actually get together.

7. Choosing the Best Solution

The art of choosing, as I define it, is the ability to understand and accept our limitations and, at the same time, take advantage of the possibilities before us.

—SHEENA IYENGAR

PURPOSE

Now that the Designer phase has resulted in a list of possible solutions for the problem/question your team has been examining, it is time to move on to the third phase of the collaborative problem-solving sequence, the Evaluator. This activity is intended to have the group evaluate the alternatives and come to consensus on the best solution(s).

PROCEDURE

1. The team leader introduces the session by referring to the easel pages of ideas that were generated during the brainstorming in Section 4 of this chapter, and indicates that the purpose of this session is to evaluate these potential solutions in order to select the ones that are likely to be most effective. The intended result is for the group to arrive at a consensus as to the best course of action. This is the phase when being an "Evaluator" is appropriate—objective, fact-based, and deliberating. Ideally, the group will accept a sense of team ownership for all the ideas that were generated and let go of attaching personal ownership for a particular idea. This will make it easier to evaluate the solutions objectively without individuals trying to protect and defend their own ideas.
2. As a group, determine if some items can be combined, clustered, or eliminated in order to simplify the list, reduce the total number, and make the list more manageable.
3. Before evaluating any of the alternatives, brainstorm what criteria would need to be met in order for a solution to be workable. Agree on criteria that are essential, and then prioritize them in terms of importance. (See *Sample Criteria for Evaluating Alternatives* at the end of this activity.)

4. Once you have a set of criteria, determine if any of the possible solutions can be eliminated because they do not meet the criteria.

5. If there are still too many possible solutions to be evaluated, reduce the number by ranking the ones that are most feasible. There are a couple of methods for doing this.

   - Divide the total number of items on the list by 3 and let each team member select that many items to keep on the list for further consideration. For example, if the total number of items is 21, everyone gets to choose the 7 alternatives that they feel are most promising. After everyone has indicated their choices, the items selected most often remain on the list and the others are eliminated.
   - Allow everyone to pick his/her top 3 choices. Weight the choices so that first choice gets 3 points, second 2, and third choice 1. Those items receiving the most points remain on the list.

6. When you have reduced the list of possible solutions, evaluate the relative merits of each by drawing a matrix with the alternative solutions down one side and the criteria across the top. Each solution is measured against the criteria to determine whether it meets them or not. The solutions that meet the greatest number of criteria are your best options.

7. If your goal is to select the one best solution, and if the criteria matrix analysis has resulted in more than one that meets the same number of criteria, then compare and contrast the few remaining options to identify the advantages and disadvantages of each. Go around the group and have team members talk about which one they like best and what they like about it.

8. If most of the group is leaning toward one of the solutions and a few team members are not yet sold on the idea, group members can address what concerns them about it. Explore whether the solution can be modified to address these concerns. See if there is a way to combine a couple of solutions so that the final outcome accommodates everyone's needs. Be persistent about crafting a win/win solution.

9. If the group is not able to come to consensus on the best solution, a follow-up session can be scheduled when the group will reconvene to decide on the matter. Discuss what could happen in the mean time to help bring the group to consensus (e.g., more research could be done, other opinions could be sought, people with concerns could return with a modified solution that would work for them, etc.).

10. As you will recall from our earlier lessons on decision-making styles, group consensus—while preferred in situations where a high degree of commitment is required to ensure the successful implementation of a decision—is not the only approach. If the group is unable to come to consensus, then it could use decision-making style 5, in which the group makes a recommendation and the leader makes the decision. In this case, the group recommendation could include a summary of the unresolved issues that blocked consensus so that all points of view can be considered by the decision maker.

Sample Criteria for Evaluating Alternatives

- The human resources necessary to successfully implement this solution are available.
- The financial resources necessary to successfully implement this solution are available.
- The technical resources necessary to successfully implement this solution are available.
- The time necessary to successfully implement this solution is available.
- The stakeholder support (from the school board, district administrators, teachers' union, parents, etc.) necessary to successfully implement this solution is available.
- The potential benefits to students are worth the possible costs involved in implementing this solution.

8. Committing To Act

*Learning is not attained by chance; it must be sought
for with ardor and attended to with diligence.*

—ABIGAIL ADAMS

PURPOSE

This is the final phase of the collaborative problem-solving process, the Activist. Now
that a solution has been identified, the purpose of this exercise is to develop a plan for
implementing that solution.

PROCEDURE

1. The team leader introduces the session by saying that now that you have evalu-
    ated your options and agreed on a solution, you are going to develop an imple-
    mentation plan that will include: what actions need to be taken, who will be
    responsible for each action, and the timeline for each step of the plan. As
    "Activists," you will act with a strong sense of commitment and determination to
    successfully implement the solution to this problem.
2. As a group, make a chart with columns headed WHAT, WHO, and WHEN.
    - Brainstorm all the action steps that need to be made in order to implement the
      plan from beginning to end. (An alternative to writing directly on the chart
      paper is to record each activity on separate sticky notes and then move the
      notes around until a logical sequence of events has been established. This can
      then be drawn into a flowchart.)
    - For each action item, have a group member sign up to be responsible for
      accomplishing it.
    - Ask the person who is responsible for completing the item what their time
      frame is.
3. Arrange to have copies of the plan distributed so that everyone has a record of
    his or her individual commitments as well as the group's overall game plan.
4. Decide how the group will monitor progress throughout the implementation of
    the plan (e.g., weekly meetings, updates via e-mail, use of an online project man-
    agement tracking tool, etc.).

9. Mastering the Art of Dilemma Management

(Or Being Between a Rock and a Hard Place)

A conscious choice must be made to deal simultaneously with both horns of a dilemma if it is to be managed and resolved.

—CAROL CARDNO

PURPOSE

An issue involving school safety arose during a coaching skills workshop I was conducting for site administrators of a Head Start program. One of the youngsters was proving to be too much of a behavior problem—biting other children and pulling their hair. The parents were complaining and the teachers wanted the child expelled. The site supervisors, frustrated by the lack of action from the central office administrators, couldn't decide what was worse: Either their leaders were clueless—weren't aware of the problem—or they were incompetent—aware of it but unable to solve it.

The real problem was that they were not dealing with a *problem* but with a *dilemma*. Viewing a situation as a problem presupposes that there is a solution. However, not every issue is a problem that can be solved with a single, discrete solution. Sometimes school leaders are confronted with a situation in which two apparently incompatible goals exist or where a necessary choice must be made between equally undesirable alternatives. In other words, you are faced with a dilemma.

In the Head Start example, there are two equally important core values to which the program is committed. One is to serve all eligible families. The other is to provide a safe, healthy, and nurturing environment for all students. To allow a child who is physically hurting other students to remain in the program is incompatible with the program's commitment to providing a safe environment. On the other hand, to expel a child who is a behavior problem could be argued to be a betrayal of the very mission of Head Start. From its inception, this federally funded program was intended to help children from disadvantaged communities learn the social skills necessary to succeed in school. Who needs this program more than the student who would be excluded?

An unacknowledged dilemma creates conflict and opposition. Dilemmas are often mistaken for a problem with a number of different interest groups attempting to arrive at a compromise solution, or as a conflict of values to be settled by a personal judgment call. Both of these will only make the situation worse and prevent finding a more satisfactory answer.

Understanding the concept of Dilemma Management frees you from the waste of energy and the consequences of poor decisions that come from trying to define every issue as a problem to be solved, as opposed to a dilemma that must be assessed and managed over time.[6]

The challenge is to shift from thinking of it as an either/or situation, and to viewing it as one paradox instead of two competing goals. In order to manage a dilemma effectively, you need to maintain the right balance so that both goals are being met to the maximum extent possible. To go too far in either direction is to risk failing at one or the other.

A successful outcome depends on a willingness to explore incremental improvements rather than seeking one fixed solution. It also requires a spirit of mutual respect and collaboration among the members of the school community as you experiment, measure results, and continuously learn together.

PROCEDURE

The Dilemma Management process consists of three key steps: identifying, analyzing, and managing the dilemma.

1. As a first step, you and your team need to be able to make the distinction between a problem, which can be solved with a single, discrete solution, and a dilemma, which has no one best solution and must be managed over time.
2. Once a dilemma has been identified, it is important for you and your team to clarify its opposing forces or polarities, and to pinpoint the upside potential and downside risks of each. Examples of a process for conducting this analysis include:

   - Articulate the organization's motivation for being committed to each of the goals. Analyze the benefits and costs of pursuing each goal.
   - List the strategies that would be used to maximize the benefits and minimize the costs of goal A.
   - List the strategies that would be used to maximize the benefits and minimize the costs of goal B.
   - Determine what would be the consequences to goal B, if goal A were pursued exclusively.
   - Determine what would be the consequences to goal A, if goal B were pursued exclusively.

   Conducting such an analysis with our Head Start program example would likely lead to the conclusion that if all children from eligible families were allowed to attend regardless of how out of control they were, then other parents would probably take their children out of the program, resulting in lost revenue and possibly loss of the program's charter to operate. On the other hand, if every student who misbehaved were to be expelled, then similar consequences of lost revenue and loss of the program's charter could result.

Clearly, it is in everyone's best interest to both serve as many eligible students as possible and to help every child learn how to act appropriately in a classroom setting so that it is safe for all students. Strategies for managing this situation might include more extensive behavior management training/coaching for staff; workshops and in-home counseling for parents; coping skills exercises with children; and referrals to community resources for diagnosis and treatment.

3. After a dilemma has been thoroughly assessed, your task is to develop specific strategies that will achieve the best of both sides of the dilemma over time. It is important to remember that dilemmas are dynamic situations and that circumstances can often require making adjustments in order to regain a sense of balance. Managing dilemmas are best done in school environments/cultures that are characterized by:

- Leaders who communicate clearly and consistently about the organization's vision, values, goals, and challenges
- Managers who have a track record of solving those problems that are, in fact, solvable
- Team members who are aligned on common goals and trust one another to be sincere in doing their best to accomplish these goals
- An organizational structure that enables open communication and effective collaboration
- A process for continuous improvement based on quantitative and qualitative assessment data

In Conclusion

The main point to remember from this part of the book is that people support what they help create.

- Coercive leadership tactics might gain you *compliance*. Collaborative leadership tactics are more likely to win you *commitment*.
- Addressing the symptoms of a problem rather than its root cause will only result in the same problem becoming more ingrained and more difficult to eradicate.
- An innovative vision without a practical plan is just wishful thinking. A practical plan without an innovative vision is just another list of things to do.
- Effective collaboration is based on an explicit agreement to respect each other and to put that respect into practice by striving to craft a solution that works for everyone.

PART FOUR

TO LEAD IS TO TEACH— COACHING SKILLS
6 Practices to Improve Performance

*Leaders are more powerful role models when
they learn than when they teach.*

—ROSBETH MOSS KANTER

Bob Beauchamp was the principal at Overland High School, and had been for 20 years. A fixture in the community, "Mr. B." was known and liked by everyone in town.

Bob enjoyed his job but had been doing it for so long that it had become pretty much routine. His real passion was buying old homes and refurbishing them. He liked working with his hands and took pride in his craftsmanship. He felt a sense of accomplishment transforming these "fixer uppers" into beautiful homes that could be resold for a handsome profit. With two college-age daughters to support, the extra income came in handy. He was only able to work on these home renovation projects on evenings, on weekends, and during the summer. He was looking forward to retiring in five years so he could do this full time.

Then, one day Bob's life changed dramatically. His school district hired a new superintendent. Ten years younger than Bob, this "hot shot" was determined to "shake things up." He called Bob into his office to inform him that his job as school principal was no longer to be an administrator, but to be an "instructional leader." Bob was told that instead of spending his days working in his office, he was to be in classrooms 80% of the time working with teachers to improve their instructional strategies.

Before becoming the principal, Bob was the high school athletics director. He was a gym teacher not a classroom teacher, and had no real subject matter expertise. The credibility he had with his staff was based on his ability to keep the school running efficiently, and on the fact that he had been around forever. The idea that he was now going to go into teachers' classrooms and show them how to be better teachers was incomprehensible to him. He felt totally unqualified and ill-equipped to handle this task.

Moving fairly quickly through the stages of denial, anger, and bargaining, Bob became severely depressed. Under a doctor's care, he took a medical leave of absence. After a few grueling weeks of self-doubt—with support from his wife and kids (along with a little coaching from me)—he decided to stop feeling like a victim of circumstances and embrace this as an opportunity to retire early and pursue his goal of refurbishing houses for love and profit.

This anecdote illustrates in a very dramatic way the challenges involved in turning school administrators into instructional leaders.

The term "instructional leader" has been in vogue since the 1980s. Based on research that identified principal leadership as essential to "instructionally effective schools," it was intended to reinforce the importance of having principals pay more attention to leading the curriculum and instructional program of the school, and spend less time focusing on "managerial" activities and bureaucratic tasks.[1]

While successful in conveying the importance of keeping teaching and learning at the forefront of decision making, "instructional leadership" proved to be less than a panacea in practice, for a number of reasons. How the role of instructional leader influenced student learning was not clearly articulated. Attempts to prove a causal relationship between instructional leadership and student achievement proved inconclusive.[2] There was also the problem reflected in the Bob Beauchamp story: Most school principals were not trained in the skills required to fulfill this new role, and the managerial activities that had previously kept them busy still needed to be done.

During the 1990s, interest in instructional leadership gave way to other models such as transformational leadership, facilitative leadership, and distributed leadership. It became clear that the principal could not do it alone. He or she did not have enough direct influence over student achievement, and the primary leadership role evolved into that of creating a "professional learning environment."

Instructional leadership was redefined in 2008 by the National Association of Elementary School Principals, which set out six standards of what principals should know and be able to do.[3] These standards emphasize the importance of schools being places of learning for both students and adults.

This part of the book is focused on your power as an educator, a teacher, and a coach. Perhaps the term "head coach" is more appropriate in describing your role as leading in the development and implementation of an effective classroom-level instructional coaching program. Whether you do the coaching personally, collaborate with teachers in designing a peer-coaching program, and/or hire a staff of coaches, the practices outlined here provide you with a structure and the skills to help teachers learn and grow.

The purpose is for you to build relationships of trust with your staff, to help them set professional development goals, to visit their classrooms and give them feedback on instructional methods and techniques, to use data to focus attention on improving the curriculum and instruction, and to support them in accessing resources and materials they need to succeed.

This section does not address your responsibility as a supervisor charged with evaluating teacher performance. The coaching approach proposed in the following lessons is clearly meant to be consultative rather than confrontational; conducted at the invitation of teachers who are interested in professional growth rather than initiated by administrators who are seeking to correct a performance problem.[4]

It should perhaps be noted that this type of in-depth coaching goes counter to the current practice of classroom walkthroughs, or what one sixth-grade teacher refers to as "Checklist Leadership."[5] Being able to get a quick snapshot of what is happening in all the classrooms has its benefits, but if the goal is to help good teachers grow into great ones, then a more sustained, committed, transparent, and empowering process is required. Ultimately, by being a source of empowerment for teachers, you will, in turn, teach them how to be a source of empowerment for students.

1. Making Deposits in the Emotional Bank Account

What we appreciate appreciates in value.

—Nan Wise

PURPOSE

For many of us, our childhood days at school helped to shape our perceptual filters to focus on what was wrong and not pay much attention to what was all right. When teachers corrected our schoolwork, they would usually put a red mark where we gave the wrong answer. All of the right answers usually went unnoticed. In a similar way, when we were behaving ourselves, we were usually left alone, but when we did something inappropriate, we would hear about it. So we tend to notice what we think is wrong and voice our complaints when things are not as we believe they should be. It takes discipline to reorient your viewfinder to pay attention to what others do right, or do well, or do to contribute in a positive way.

Think of it as making deposits into an "emotional bank account." If you are consistently acknowledging the other person, expressing appreciation for all the many things—big and small—that he or she does to make your work lives together more pleasant and productive, you build up a healthy account of positive "deposits." Then when he or she does something about which you feel you have a legitimate complaint, and you say something negative—essentially making a "withdrawal" from the account—the relationship will not go "bankrupt."

Stating appreciations should not be attempts to manipulate or get something—this is not a behavior-modification technique. Rather, it's an opportunity to be sincere in sharing what you appreciate in your coworkers. Very few people respond well to criticism. Almost everyone blossoms when they feel appreciated.

The purpose of this exercise is to get you in the habit of acknowledging positive contributions before you provide any feedback that might be received by them as negative. Conventional wisdom suggests it takes 21 to 30 days of doing something repeatedly before it becomes a habit.

We are what we repeatedly do. Excellence then,
is not an act, but a habit.

—ARISTOTLE

PROCEDURE

The goal is to make at least one weekly "deposit into the emotional bank account" of each of your colleagues. To support you in keeping track of your efforts, create a spreadsheet by listing the names of colleagues down the left-hand side of the page. Then, make four columns to the right of the names with week 1, week 2, week 3, and week 4 across the top. When you deliver positive feedback to a staff person, put a checkmark next to his or her name. Continue doing this for the next four weeks, or until it has become a habit.

In order for feedback to be meaningful to the recipient, it needs to be *sincere*. Even though you are doing this as an exercise, it shouldn't come across as phony; otherwise, it would be counterproductive. Look for things that staff members do that really matter to you, and really make a difference to the school, and be authentic in expressing your appreciation.

Feedback is more effective when it is *specific*. Rather than a vague, general comment such as "Good job," describe in detail what the person did that you think merits recognition.

For example,

> *I very much appreciated the question you asked during the staff meeting. It helped me clarify the point I was trying to make.*

> *I noticed how you intervened with the two students in the playground who were arguing over whose turn it was. I think you handled the situation in a way that taught the students how to resolve differences with respect.*

If you know the communication style of your colleagues, then you can customize your feedback so that it has maximum positive impact. Here are some guidelines for you to follow.

Conscientious

Describe the specific, concrete, tangible step your colleague took that worked.

For example,

> *Writing the objective of the lesson on the board and then reading it aloud really helped students understand what they were expected to learn.*

Creative

Acknowledge what was unique, special, and innovative about how the teacher did it.

For example,

> *Having a full-length mirror and a box of old clothes was such a clever way of teaching language arts to your class of hearing-impaired first-graders. They loved playing dress-up and had fun learning how to say and sign different words such as "hat," "shoes," and "scarf."*

Competitive

Focus on what results and measurable outcomes were accomplished.
For example,

> *Test scores show that your students are the top performers among fourth-graders.*
> *Your persistence in challenging them to work hard and not letting them give up until they have solved the problem correctly is really paying off.*

Collaborative

Share what personal attribute and "human touch" made a difference.
For example,

> *Making eye contact with students and greeting each of them by name when they come into your classroom is such a nice way of letting them know you care about them. It is no wonder that they are so well behaved.*

2. Creating a Context for Coaching

Coaching is the process of enabling others to act, of building on their strengths. It's counting on other people to use their special skill and competence, and then giving them enough room and enough time to do it.

—TOM PETERS

PURPOSE

According to *HR Monthly*, "Recent studies show business coaching and executive coaching to be the most effective means for achieving sustainable growth, change and development in the individual, group and organization."

A coach is not an umpire. A coach is on the same team as the players and invested in their success. Whereas, an umpire evaluates the players' performance, and rules who is "safe" and who is "out." This is an important distinction because your role as an instructional leader can be better served if your staff feels as if you are on their side, and not just there to catch them making an error.

The nature or context of the relationship is different when school leaders are *coaching* teachers than when they are *evaluating* them. To make the point clear and establish the appropriate framework for the practices in this section, you are invited to think of the teachers you are or will be coaching as your "clients."

The purpose of this next series of lessons is to help you build relationships with teachers that nurture, motivate, and empower them by enhancing their skills and by helping them channel the time and resources they need to achieve their professional development goals. The qualifications you need to succeed as a coach include:

- Ability to serve as a role model by maintaining an overall positive attitude and professional manner.
- Good people skills with an ability to listen to teachers as clients and help them reflect on progress toward achieving their goals.
- Well-organized with a proven track record of goal achievement.

- Willing to be available and flexible in meeting the individual needs of teachers as clients, while balancing your own needs and priorities.
- Commitment to continuous education/professional development through training and coaching.

PROCEDURE

1. Meet with your colleagues to discuss the purpose of coaching, the potential benefits to them and their students, and the respective roles of the coach and the "client."

Purpose and Benefits of Coaching

- Coaching is an opportunity for the school leader as coach and teacher as client to work together to improve classroom instruction in support of student success.
- Coaching provides a structure for individual teachers to set professional development goals based on an honest assessment of strengths and weaknesses.
- Coaching creates a safe space for teachers to practice new instructional strategies and to build additional teaching skills with the supportive guidance of a trusted colleague.
- Coaching gives school leaders a means for having direct, positive influence on the teaching/learning environment.

Role of the Coach

- Build relationships with teachers as clients based on trust, mutual respect, nonjudgmental interactions, and clear and appropriate boundaries.
- Assist teachers as clients in taking effective action toward achieving their goals by using coaching tools including listening actively; asking reflective questions; matching communication styles; solving problems; and setting goals, objectives, action plans, and timelines.
- Help teachers as clients access the resources they need to accomplish their goals.
- Be willing to give and receive honest feedback.
- Keep all information shared in the utmost confidence.

Role of the Teacher As Client

- Take responsibility for getting value out of the coaching process and for learning as much as you can about yourself, and about becoming a more effective teacher.
- Be present, punctual, and prepared for coaching sessions.
- Complete assigned exercises and homework and keep commitments that you make.
- Be willing to give and receive honest feedback.

2. Review the steps involved in the coaching process and address any questions that arise.

Steps in the Coaching Process

- Teacher sets a goal. Coach asks questions and helps ensure that the goal is realistic.
- Teacher develops an action plan. Coach asks questions and may offer suggestions.
- Teacher implements the action plan in the classroom. Coach observes the teacher in the classroom and may lend support to the teacher during the lesson. Coach takes notes in preparation for providing feedback.
- Teacher studies the results of the classroom interaction. Coach asks reflective questions and provides feedback on what worked and what could be improved. Teacher works with the coach to revise the action plan based on lessons learned.
- Teacher implements the revised plan in the classroom. Coach observes and takes notes.
- Teacher and coach meet to discuss how the revised plan worked and how these strategies or skills can be applied to other classroom situations.

3. The purpose of having a coaching contract is to make sure that expectations are clear from the outset. Review the *School Leader As Coach/Teacher As Client: Sample Coaching Contract* and collaborate on any changes staff would like to make in order for the contract to work for them.

School Leader As Coach/Teacher As Client: Sample Coaching Contract

---

Teacher As Client Understandings

I understand that coaching is designed to be a nurturing, motivating, and empowering experience that builds on my strengths, enhances my skills, and helps me channel the time and resources I need to achieve my professional development goals.

I understand that coaching is not part of the formal teacher evaluation process and that— for the duration of this contract—my coach is functioning as my partner, not my supervisor.

Teacher As Client Agreements

1. *I understand and agree that I am fully responsible for my well-being throughout the coaching process. I understand that I am in charge of the choices I make, and the results I achieve. I agree to take full responsibility for all actions that I take as a result of coaching.*
2. *I agree to be honest about what I want to achieve, about the challenges and obstacles I face, and about my confidence in being able to meet my goals.*
3. *I agree to take responsibility for generating my own solutions and resolving my own problems.*

(continues)

School Leader As Coach/Teacher As Client: Sample Coaching Contract, *continued*

4. *I agree to keep the commitments I make toward working on my goals.*
5. *I agree to be present, punctual, and prepared for my coaching sessions.*
6. *I agree to complete assigned exercises and homework. I understand that a pattern of my not completing assignments may be viewed as a lack of commitment on my part, which could result in termination of the coaching process.*
7. *I understand that successful coaching depends on honest communication. I will share honest feedback with my coach and ask that my coach do the same. If the sessions aren't working for me, I agree to say something so we can adjust our working style.*

School Leader As Coach Agreements

1. *As a coach, I agree to support you in achieving the goals you set for yourself.*
2. *I agree to help you develop the skills you wish to master.*
3. *I agree to assist you in accessing the resources you need to accomplish your goals.*
4. *I agree to treat you with respect and consideration.*
5. *I agree to be honest with you in giving you feedback about your progress, in making observations about the process, and in communicating any limits on my ability to be helpful or available in responding to any specific requests.*
6. *I agree to keep all information shared in the utmost confidence.*

Coaching process start date _____ and end date _____

Our signatures on this contract indicate full understanding of and agreement with the information outlined above.

Teacher As Client

Signature:_____ Date_____

School Leader As Coach

Signature:_____ Date_____

3. Coaching BOLD Goals

First Coaching Session

*Those who have achieved all their aims probably
set them too low.*

—Herbert von Karajan

PURPOSE

The purpose of step 1 in the coaching process is for the teacher to choose a professional development goal that will serve as the focus of your coaching interactions. This lesson combines BOLD goals and effective questioning techniques to provide you with a structure for your first coaching session.

PROCEDURE

1. Schedule a 30- to 40-minute meeting with each of the teachers you will be coaching. In preparation for this first coaching session, ask the teachers to come prepared to discuss with you the professional development goals they would like to achieve this year. Suggest that as part of their goal-identification process, they might want to consider recent performance evaluations, data collected on student achievement, and/or schoolwide goals.
2. Start the coaching session with a review of the context of coaching material covered in step 2 at the previous staff meeting, and have a copy of the *School Leader As Coach/Teacher As Client: Sample Coaching Contract* for you and the teacher to sign.
3. Use the following *Goal Setting Guidelines: Sample Coaching Questions* as a framework for the goal-setting process.

To be a goal, it must be within your control.

Goal-Setting Guidelines: Sample Coaching Questions

BOLD ENOUGH TO BE A STRETCH

Open-Ended Questions: Ask a broad question to invite the teacher to consider a range of possibilities before focusing on a single goal. Here are some examples of open-ended questions:

- *What goals would you like to achieve this year that you feel will improve your teaching?*
- *Where do you see some opportunities to enhance your ability to encourage student success?*

Clarifying Questions: Using something the teacher said in answer to your open-ended questions, ask clarifying questions to probe further toward narrowing in on a specific goal. Here are some examples:

- *You've identified three possible goals for this year. Which one do you think would make the biggest difference?*
- *When you talk about doing a more effective job at meeting the individual needs of all students, what exactly do you have in mind?*

Summarizing Questions: When you believe the teacher has a clear sense of the goal on which he or she wants to focus, confirm your mutual understanding by asking a summarizing question. Here are some examples:

- *Are you saying that of the possible goals you considered, the one you think would make the biggest difference is your learning to develop lessons that challenge students to do more high-level thinking?*
- *So the way you could imagine better meeting the needs of individual students is to vary instruction methods including the idea of incorporating more inquiry-based learning in your lessons. Is that correct?*

OBJECTIVELY MEASURABLE

Open-Ended Questions: Begin the process of determining how progress on the goal can be measured. Here are some sample open-ended questions:

- *How will you measure if your lessons are challenging students to do more high-level thinking?*
- *How will you measure if your inquiry-based lessons are meeting the needs of your students?*

Clarifying Questions: Once again, using something the teacher said in answer to your open-ended questions, ask clarifying questions to probe further to define how success will be measured. Here are some examples:

- *What evidence would you have that higher-level thinking is occurring?*
- *What tools are available for measuring higher-level thinking?*
- *How do you currently measure the extent to which you are meeting the individual needs of students?*
- *What indicators will you have that you are being more effective in meeting the needs of all students?*

Goal-Setting Guidelines: Sample Coaching Questions, *continued*

Summarizing Questions: When you think the teacher has a clear sense of how to measure success, confirm your mutual understanding by asking a summarizing question. Here are some examples:

- *Do I have this right? You will use the Revised Bloom's Taxonomy as a structure for planning your lessons, and for measuring student progress from simply remembering facts to being able to perform higher levels of analysis and synthesis.*
- *So, as a first step in determining the individual needs of your students, you will do an assessment of each student's preferred learning style. Correct?*

LINKED TO PROFESSIONAL OR SCHOOL IMPROVEMENT PLAN

Open-Ended Questions: Ask questions to put this one goal in the broader context of the teacher's professional development plan, or the school's improvement plan.

- *How does this goal fit into the three goals identified in your Individual Growth Plan?*
- *To which of the five schoolwide goals is your goal most closely aligned?*

Clarifying Questions

- *So you're saying that as part of your most recent performance evaluation process, you received feedback that this was a growth area for you. Is that right?*
- *You see that varying instructional methods to meet the needs of individual students is critical to closing the achievement gap between the general student population and students in target groups, which is Goal 1 in our school plan. Do I understand you correctly?*

Summarizing Questions

- *This is one of the three goals you committed to work on this year, and you believe this is the one you should focus on first. Correct?*
- *Are you comfortable that you've chosen a goal that will contribute to the school's overall plan?*

DATE-SPECIFIC

Open-Ended Questions

- *How much time will it take you to have a system in place for using the Revised Bloom's Taxonomy on a consistent basis?*
- *How long will it take you to do the Learning Styles assessment with your students?*

Clarifying Questions

- *Once you have a system in place, how long before you will be ready for me to come into your classroom and observe a lesson you have prepared using this tool?*
- *If you can complete the assessment by the end of next week, then how soon after that should I plan on visiting your classroom so that I can see how you are varying your instructional methods?*

Summarizing Questions

- *So, in three weeks we should plan on my scheduling time to visit your classroom. Will you confirm a time with me at the beginning of that week?*
- *The week after next, then, should be a good time for me to come in to observe your lesson. Is that what we're saying?*

4. Giving Focused Feedback

Second Coaching Session

*In an effective classroom students should not only
know what they are doing, they should also know
why and how.*

—HARRY WONG

PURPOSE

Here is another opportunity for you to apply the **Plan-Do-Study-Act (PDSA) Cycle** at
school, this time in your role as coach. At the first coaching session with your teacher,
he or she sets a professional development goal. The process continues with the teacher
creating a **Plan** for implementing that goal in the classroom, and then for him or her to
Do it with your being there as an observer. Together, you and the teacher will **Study** the
effectiveness of the plan so that the teacher can **Act** to refine the lesson and extend its
use for teaching other skills and concepts.

The purpose of this exercise is for you and the teacher to collaborate on the pro-
tocol to be used for your providing constructive feedback based on your observing
him or her in the classroom.

PROCEDURE

1. In preparation for your second coaching session, provide the teacher with the
   template for the *Classroom Observation Feedback Form*, and ask him or her to
   complete this and bring it to your next coaching session. The first section of the
   form is for summarizing the BOLD goal identified at your first coaching session.
   Next, the teacher will articulate the learning objectives and teaching strategies
   involved in implementing this goal in the classroom.

   The second section of the form is to delineate what an observer could be
   expected to see if the teacher's instructional strategies are successful in achieving
   the objectives. Specifically, from the viewpoint of an observer, what would you
   expect to see in terms of teacher behavior, student behavior, as well as the classroom environment? Here are some sample indicators of success.

What you would expect to observe on the part of the teacher? For example,

- Communicates to students *WHAT* is being taught.
- Communicates to students *HOW* they will be engaged in learning the skills and concepts.
- Communicates to students *WHY* the skills and concepts are being taught.
- Links this lesson to previously taught skills and concepts.
- Structures the presentation of the material in ways that address multiple learning styles.
- Directs and motivates each student so that all students are engaged.
- Interacts with students in a positive manner while keeping them on task.
- Asks students questions to assess their degree of comprehension.

What you would expect to observe on the part of students? For example,

- Listens to the teacher's instructions.
- Asks questions that help clarify the *WHAT*, *HOW*, and/or *WHY* of the lesson.
- Stays on task at least 80% of the time.
- Answers higher-order questions.
- Connects the lesson to real-world examples.
- Completes the assignment successfully.

What you would expect to observe about the physical environment? For example,

- Room is set up in a way that supports the instructional objectives of this lesson.
- Visual material that is relevant to this lesson is on the walls.
- Student work—especially examples of related lessons— is displayed.
- Manipulatives to aid in the teaching of this lesson are available.
- Technology to aid in the teaching of this lesson is available.
- Distractions are kept to a minimum.

2. Complete the form yourself prior to the next coaching session so that you and the teacher can compare expectations.

3. At the second coaching session, share each other's proposed Feedback Observation Forms, and discuss expectations that the two of you have in common. Also, discuss any expectations that appear only on his or her list or only on yours, and agree on which of these ought to be included as indicators of success. You should end up with one final set of items that you both agree are the areas to be focused on during the classroom observation.

4. Arrange to visit the teacher's classroom at a time that works for both of you. Use this feedback form to record your observations, which you will share with the teacher at the next coaching session. Establish ahead of time how you will or will not interact with the teacher and students while you are observing in the classroom, where you will sit, and how your presence will be explained to the students.

Classroom Observation Feedback Form

BOLD Goal:

•

Learning Objectives:

•

•

•

Teaching Strategies:

•

•

•

Observable Indicators of Success:

What you would expect to observe on the part of the teacher?

•

•

•

•

What you would expect to observe on the part of students?

•

•

•

•

What you would expect to observe about the physical environment?

•

•

•

•

•

5. Balancing Reflection and Instruction

Third Coaching Session

*It is not so much where my motivation comes from
but rather how it manages to survive*

—LOUISE BOURGEOIS

PURPOSE

The literature on coaching makes distinctions among various types of coaching strategies, claiming that effective coaches are able to blend different strategies into their practice.[6] In this lesson—which provides you with the structure for your third coaching session—you will use both facilitative and instructional coaching strategies. Facilitative coaching focuses on building the teacher's capacity to reflect, analyze, synthesize, and create new and improved ways of educating students. In contrast, instructional coaching includes the expectation that you will provide perspective, input, and suggestions based on your expertise and experience.

The purpose of this coaching session is to study how much progress the teacher is making on achieving his or her professional development goals based on how well the lesson went with the students in his or her class.

PROCEDURE

1. Schedule this coaching session as soon as possible after your classroom observation.
2. The teacher being observed will come prepared with the following observations:
   - What worked? What factors contributed to what worked?
   - What didn't work as well as expected? What factors contributed to what didn't work?
   - What will you do differently next time to continue to improve?

3. Prior to this session, review the notes you took on the feedback form during your classroom observation, and organize your thoughts along the lines of the three questions posed to the teacher.

4. Start the session by asking for the teacher's observations. Use reflective questions designed to expand the teacher's awareness, inspire greater insight, deepen understanding, help internalize the learning, and promote clearer comprehension of where to go from here. (Use the *Facilitative Coaching Strategies: Reflective Questions Worksheet* provided.)

5. Share your observations and give feedback that validates the teacher's observations, adds another perspective, reveals possible blind-spots in the teacher's view, suggests alternative ways of interpreting events or data, and provides a structure for integrating the reflections and suggestions so that the teacher feels confident in his or her ability to act on the lessons learned from the coaching experience. (Use the *Instructional Coaching Strategies: Giving and Receiving Feedback* guidelines provided.)

6. Together, the coach and the teacher can create an action plan for refining his or her teaching strategies in preparation for a second classroom observation.

7. Schedule a second classroom observation, and agree on the areas of focus. Collaborate on the questions the two of you will explore at your final coaching session.

8. Use this same structure for your final coaching session.

Facilitative Coaching Strategies: Reflective Questions Worksheet

---

QUESTION AREA 1—WHAT WORKED?

Open-Ended Questions

• *What worked?*

• *What factors contribute to what worked?*

Clarifying Questions

• *How do you know it worked? What evidence/data do you have?*

• *What specific things did you do that worked to keep the students engaged?*

Facilitative Coaching Strategies: Reflective Questions Worksheet, *continued*

- *What is an example of how one of your students asked a question revealing higher-order thinking?*

- *How did the time you spent planning the lesson pay off for you?*

- *Specifically, how did your use of technology improve student comprehension?*

Summarizing Questions

- *Is it true to say that you are generally pleased with how well the lesson worked?*

- *Sounds like you have discovered some new tools to use that will enable you to be more effective in meeting the needs of all students. Would you agree?*

QUESTION AREA 2—WHAT DIDN'T WORK?

Open-Ended Questions

- *What didn't work as well as expected?*

- *What factors contributed to what didn't work?*

Clarifying Questions

- *What exactly were you expecting, and how did this fall short?*

- *What evidence/data do you have that suggests this didn't fully accomplish what you had hoped?*

(*continues*)

Facilitative Coaching Strategies: Reflective Questions Worksheet, *continued*

- *What example do you have that demonstrates how this could have worked better?*

- *To what do you attribute your less than completely successful attempt?*

- *What surprised you about the difficulty some students had with the lesson?*

Summarizing Questions

- *Even though there were things that definitely worked, you've also identified some areas that you could improve. Correct?*

- *Are you ready to build on what you've learned, and move onto defining what changes you could make next time?*

QUESTION AREA 3—WHAT WILL YOU DO DIFFERENTLY NEXT TIME?

Open-Ended Questions

- *What lessons did you learn from what worked? What lessons did you learn from what didn't work as well as expected?*

- *Given what you've learned, what will you do differently next time to continue to improve?*

Clarifying Questions

- *So it worked to have a well-developed lesson plan. Any changes you would make to the planning process?*

Facilitative Coaching Strategies: Reflective Questions Worksheet, *continued*

- *It worked to start this lesson with a clear statement of WHAT, HOW, and WHY. Will you use that next time as well?*

- *You've determined that it didn't work to. . . What adjustments will you make next time?*

- *What else could you do so that the students who had difficulty with the lesson this time will be able to understand and complete the task next time?*

Summarizing Questions

- *After reflecting on what worked and what didn't, you've identified two areas to focus on that you believe will improve the lesson. Do I have that right?*

- *You seem to have a good grasp of what needs to be done for you to achieve your goal. Is that true?*

Instructional Coaching Strategies: Giving and Receiving Feedback

Validate the Teacher's Self-Assessment

- Restate an observation the teacher made with which you agree, and use this to reinforce the teacher's capacity to self-correct.
- Reinforce, wherever possible, the teacher's analysis of the relevant factors, and underscore the key learnings to be derived from the experience.

Offer Your Assessment

- Use the structure created by the two of you for the Feedback Form to give feedback on what you observed on the part of the teacher, what you observed on the part of the students, and what you observed about the physical environment relevant to the lesson.
- Focus on specific behaviors using examples of what you observed.
- Describe the consequences or impact of the teacher's behaviors on student behaviors.

(continues)

Instructional Coaching Strategies: Giving and Receiving Feedback, *continued*

- Use language that is descriptive rather than judgmental.
  For example: *When you asked if any of the students had any questions, even though none of them raised their hands, I observed that a few of them asked other students what they were supposed to do.*
  As compared to: *It showed bad judgment on your part to assume that none of the students had any questions before you moved on to the next instruction.*
- Ask the teacher to reflect on your assessment.

Collaborate on an Action Plan

- Review what worked, what didn't work, and what lessons were learned.
- Discuss what changes the teacher will make in preparation for your observing him or her present the revised lesson in the classroom.
- Offer suggestions and recommendations based on your observations and experience.
- Decide if there should be any changes in terms of how you function as a coach during the lesson (i.e., Do you remain a silent observer, do you co-teach the lesson, do you model how to handle a certain part of the lesson, etc.).

Invite Feedback on Your Coaching

- Let the teacher know that you would appreciate receiving feedback on how the coaching process is working so far.
- Ask for specific examples of the coaching exchanges that have been especially helpful.
- Ask for specific examples of the coaching exchanges that have been less than fully helpful.
- Ask how you could increase the value the teacher is receiving from the coaching process.
- Restate the suggestions the teacher has made for improving the coaching process.
- Confirm what you will do differently in the future to improve the coaching relationship based on his or her feedback.

6. Sharing Best Practices

Leadership should be born out of the understanding
of the needs of those who would be affected by it.

—MARIAN ANDERSON

PURPOSE

This lesson is an opportunity for you to use the data you've collected through the coaching sessions you've conducted and the classroom observations you've made to conduct a staff meeting intended to develop schoolwide goals and action plans.

PROCEDURE

1. Start the meeting by sharing "best practices" observed during your classroom observations. Posting your key findings on flip chart pages so that they can be seen by all staff and referred to during the meeting is a good way to present this information.
2. Next, encourage staff to consider how to strengthen and expand these effective strategies more broadly throughout the school. You could do this as a brainstorming session.
3. Having acknowledged what's working well in the classrooms, it is now time to ask the staff to reflect on what's not working as effectively. Report areas in need of improvement that you observed in multiple classrooms suggesting a schoolwide response would be appropriate. Once again, posting these would be helpful. Using charts and graphs to present data is often the best way to illustrate the scale or scope of a problem, as well as to reveal patterns and trends.
4. Now brainstorm ideas for how the school community can work together to address the classroom practices identified as needing improvement. You might find some of the collaboration skills included in Part Three to be useful during this process.
5. Work together to select one or two ideas from both brainstormed lists—one to expand best practices and one to improve an area of weakness—by having each staff person put a check mark or other notation next to the one idea in each list he or she thinks should be implemented.

6. Break into two to four teams to develop action plans.
7. Each team can present its action plans to the full group using flip charts to outline what actions will be taken, by whom, and in what timeframe.
8. Agree on a date by when the teams will report back to the full group on progress that has been made in implementing these plans.

In Conclusion

The main point to remember from this part of the book is that the single most important school-based factor in student success is teacher effectiveness. High achievers in many different professions from athletes to business executives count on coaches to help them improve their performance.

- Effective coaches measure their success based on how successful their clients are in achieving their goals.
- Effective coaches study what works for each of their individual clients and adapt their coaching style accordingly.
- Effective coaches blend *asking* with *telling*, *facilitating* with *instructing*. They empower their clients by allowing them to succeed based on what they know, and to not fail based on what they don't.

PART FIVE

TO LEAD IS TO SUCCEED— CONTINUOUS IMPROVEMENT SKILLS
6 Steps to Manage Change

I change myself,
I change the world.

—GLORIA ANZALDUA

A widely referred to model details (with more than a touch of irony) the six phases of a project. They are:

1. Enthusiasm
2. Disillusionment
3. Panic
4. Search for the guilty
5. Punishment of the innocent
6. Praise and honors for the nonparticipants

As schools go through the process of implementing reform strategies and improvement plans, administrators and staff often start off being enthusiastic about the possibility of making real change. Since research suggests that at least half of these reform efforts fail, it is easy to understand why school improvement teams become disillusioned. Panic would not be an inappropriate response to the prospect of the principal and teachers being fired for failing to increase student achievement. Thus, the guilty have been found and punished. Enter the new team. Return to phase 1.

The purpose of Part Five is to avoid this cycle of failure by providing a framework for how to manage change and sustain continuous improvement over time. Below is a *Leadership for Change* chart that explains the five fundamental factors that support successful change in organizations, along with the results that occur when all five are not in place.

Your school and/or district probably has a mission statement. You may also have a vision and set of core values or beliefs. All these are essential, but not sufficient. A mission/vision without the other change factors leads to cynicism because it's clear that leadership is not really serious or committed to following through on the rhetoric.

As one cynical educator claimed at one of my workshops, "The way to be at the forefront of educational innovation is to resist change long enough. Sooner or later the pendulum of school reform movements will come swinging back."

Regardless of the direction in which school improvement efforts are headed, the point is that improvement is continuous and change is constant. During the process of change, new things will be tried, mistakes will be made, and hopefully, lessons will be learned. On any given day, school staff members may find themselves confident or confused, motivated or deflated.

The purpose of this part is to help you navigate through the often turbulent and sometimes treacherous waters of change by deepening your understanding of the five foundations for successfully leading organizational change.

Table 5.1 *Leadership for Change* is a good way of understanding why so many attempts at school reform and organizational change fail.

The first foundation for change is **vision**, which most schools have. While it's important to have a vision, it is not sufficient. Without a plan for how to achieve the vision, you don't produce change; you produce cynicism, which is an understandable reaction to what is perceived to be leadership that is all talk and no action.

The next row on the chart shows what happens if you add the second foundation, an **action plan**, which again most schools have. As critical as school improvement plans are, the result will be false starts without the resources necessary to support and sustain these efforts.

Row three illustrates that anxiety is the logical outcome of a change process that includes only the first three foundations. With a vision, plan, and **resources**,

TABLE 5.1 Leadership for Change

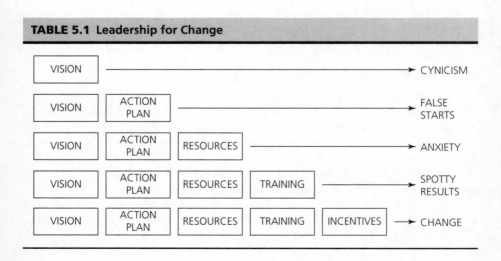

expectations are high that staff can begin to effect the desired changes. However, **training** and coaching will be required for staff to become competent and confident in their ability to perform in new ways.

Finally, the **incentives**, rewards, and recognition need to be aligned with the desired change. If, for example, the school wants to change to a form of "authentic assessment" such as portfolios, and yet the teachers' effectiveness is measured by standardized test scores, then most teachers will continue to focus on the standardized measures. Only those who are passionately dedicated to the change will persevere, and the results will be spotty, at best.

This section of the book will help you implement a process for continuous improvement at your school by giving you a framework and the tools for securing the five foundations for leading change successfully.

1. Creating a Culture of Shared Leadership

You don't manage people, you manage things.
You lead people.

—REAR ADMIRAL GRACE HOPPER

PURPOSE

Much of the literature on leadership development tends to promote the concept of "leader as hero" where one charismatic, transformational person single-handedly drives the team/company/organization/political party to victory. While we would all commend the heroic efforts of Captain Chesley "Sully" Sullenberger in successfully ditching US Airways Flight 1549 into the Hudson River and saving the lives of all 155 people on the aircraft, and we would all wish for a leader with his "Captain Cool" demeanor, his decisiveness, and his decades of training and experience the next time we are in a crisis, he would be the first to admit he didn't do it alone. Captain Sullenberger acknowledged that he and his co-pilot worked as a team. Recognition was also given to the rest of the flight crew, the passengers, the first responders, and the air traffic controller.

The role of a powerful leader as a catalyst for turning around troubled schools is well documented. At the same time, schools have come to embrace the "distributed leadership" model, which is designed to create a culture of shared leadership, because the "leader as hero" model is neither sustainable nor is it optimal. Not only are there not enough highly qualified education leaders to head every school in the country, but also the job of running a school has become too complex for any one person to do alone. Tapping into the experience, skills, and passion of talented teachers, along with that of other staff and administrators, parents and community leaders, and even students, just makes good sense.

One of the contributions that has been made by the development of the distributed leadership model is to expand the focus from leaders to leadership, and to move beyond the *leadership actions* of individual school leaders to the *leadership interactions* of a team or community. Then the intriguing question becomes: If school leadership (however we define or structure it) were successful at our site, what *leadership outcomes* would be manifest?

The purpose of this and the next five lessons is to give you a structure for creating and sustaining effective change by promoting leadership interactions throughout the school.

PROCEDURE

1. Read through the *Leadership Outcomes Leadership Actions (Self-Assessment) Worksheet*, where you will see that the five foundations for successfully leading organizational change have been translated into leadership outcomes.
2. For each of the leadership outcomes, determine how you would measure the effectiveness of your leadership actions and fill in the appropriate space on the worksheet. Sample measures are provided.
3. Rate your current level of effectiveness using the five-point scale.
4. Identify Improvement Strategies in two areas:
   • What can you do in your leadership role to model and monitor this outcome?
   • What can you do to create a culture of shared leadership that will encourage ownership among members of your school community to actively support this outcome?

Leadership Outcomes Leadership Actions (Self-Assessment) Worksheet

---

1. MISSION/VISION
Leadership Outcome
All stakeholders share and support a vision of learning, which they helped develop and are involved in implementing.

Current Assessment
How effective have my actions been in articulating and communicating my vision, as measured by

Examples:
• *How many times I've communicated it at staff meetings, in the school newsletter, at parent nights, etc.*
• *How much of my vision has been incorporated into the school's vision statement*
• *How many ways I monitor aspects of my vision in action on a daily basis so that students and staff know I mean what I say about what matters*

Rating
5 = Highly effective, 4 = Very effective, 3 = Moderately effective, 2 = Somewhat effective, 1 = Not effective

---

(*continues*)

Leadership Outcomes Leadership Actions (Self-Assessment) Worksheet, *continued*

Improvement Strategy

What more can I do in my leadership role to model and monitor this outcome?

What more can I do to create a culture of shared leadership that will encourage ownership among members of my school community to actively support this outcome?

2. GOALS/STRATEGIES/ACTION PLANS

Leadership Outcome

All stakeholders share and support a set of strategic goals and action plans aimed at increasing student achievement, which they helped develop and are involved in implementing.

Current Assessment

How effective have my actions been in holding myself accountable for achieving my BOLD goals, as measured by

Examples:
- *How many of my goals I've successfully achieved each month*
- *How many months I've continued to post new goals*
- *How many staff members have also gotten into the habit of posting BOLD goals*

Rating
5 = Highly effective, 4 = Very effective, 3 = Moderately effective, 2 = Somewhat effective, 1 = Not effective

Improvement Strategy

What more can I do in my leadership role to model and monitor this outcome?

What more can I do to create a culture of shared leadership that will encourage ownership among members of my school community to actively support this outcome?

**Leadership Outcomes Leadership Actions (Self-Assessment)
Worksheet,** *continued*

3. RESOURCES

Leadership Outcome
Sufficient resources are available and allocated in alignment with the school's commitment to student achievement.

Current Assessment
How effective have my actions been in identifying and acquiring the resources I need to succeed, as measured by

Examples:
- *How much more time I've been able to spend on instructional rather than administrative tasks*
- *How much additional support I've been able get for our school from the district*
- *How much additional support I've been able get for our school from parents and the business community*

Rating
*5 = Highly effective, 4 = Very effective, 3 = Moderately effective, 2 = Somewhat effective,
1 = Not effective*

Improvement Strategy
What more can I do in my leadership role to model and monitor this outcome?

What more can I do to create a culture of shared leadership that will encourage ownership among members of my school community to actively support this outcome?

4. TRAINING

Leadership Outcome
All staff members are participating in a professional development program focused on effective teaching and learning, which they helped design and evaluate.

(*continues*)

Leadership Outcomes Leadership Actions (Self-Assessment) Worksheet, *continued*

Current Assessment
How effective have my actions been in participating in professional development training and coaching to develop the skills I need to succeed, as measured by

Examples:
- *How much progress I've made in achieving the learning outcomes I identified at the beginning of this book*
- *How much time I've spent in training with staff to improve curriculum and instruction*
- *How many relevant tools and practices I've learned by working with a mentor or coach*

Rating
5 = Highly effective, 4 = Very effective, 3 = Moderately effective, 2 = Somewhat effective, 1 = Not effective

Improvement Strategy
What more can I do in my leadership role to model and monitor this outcome?

What more can I do to create a culture of shared leadership that will encourage ownership among members of my school community to actively support this outcome?

5. INCENTIVES

Leadership Outcome
All members of the school community are genuinely motivated, and experience a high level of job satisfaction because they see their efforts paying off in ways that are measurable for students, and rewarding for them.

Current Assessment
How effective have my actions been in ensuring that I structure my work so that I experience the benefits outweighing the costs, as measured by

Leadership Outcomes Leadership Actions (Self-Assessment) Worksheet, *continued*

Examples:
- *How much I enjoy coming to work every day*
- *How much satisfaction I experience when I observe students really engaged in learning*
- *How little time I spend wishing I were somewhere else*

Rating

5 = Highly effective, 4 = Very effective, 3 = Moderately effective, 2 = Somewhat effective, 1 = Not effective

Improvement Strategy

What more can I do in my leadership role to model and monitor this outcome?

What more can I do to create a culture of shared leadership that will encourage ownership among members of my school community to actively support this outcome?

2. Envisioning School Success

*Dissatisfaction and discouragement are not caused by
the absence of things but the absence of vision.*

—ANONYMOUS

PURPOSE

The purpose of this and the next series of lessons is to identify and implement leadership interactions that will create and sustain the five foundations for successfully leading organizational change. The first of those is a clear and compelling mission/vision. A mission statement establishes what "business" you are in—the most fundamental reason for your organization's existence.

Your school probably already has a mission and/or vision statement. Part One of this lesson is an opportunity for your team to assess how well the mission/vision statement is working, and to develop some improvement strategies to keep the vision alive.

Part Two of this lesson is a team activity that will deepen your team's shared understanding of who you are, what you do, where you're going, and why it matters.

PROCEDURE: PART ONE

1. Using the decision-making styles model in Part Three, decide how you will decide who should be involved in the leadership interactions for each of these five outcomes. Consider whether it would be best to have one consistent group, such as the School Site Council or School Improvement Team, be solely involved throughout the process, and/or to have more flexible ad hoc teams take on aspects of the process.
2. Present the model of the five foundations for successfully leading organizational change and discuss with the team the implications for achieving continuous improvement at the school.
3. Read the leadership outcome for the first foundation noted on the *Leadership Outcomes Leadership Interactions (Team-Assessment) Mission/Vision Worksheet.*
4. Now have the team conduct an assessment of the current situation using the suggested criteria from the worksheet as a guide.
5. Finally, the team is to design Improvement Strategies for ensuring that this leadership outcome is strengthened and sustained.

Leadership Outcomes Leadership Interactions (Team-Assessment) Mission/Vision Worksheet

---

Leadership Outcome
All stakeholders share and support a vision of learning, which they helped develop and are involved in implementing.

Current Assessment (Suggested Criteria)

- How well does our school's vision communicate our central focus on student learning?

- What evidence do we have that all stakeholders share and support our vision?

- How many stakeholders helped develop our vision?

- How many stakeholders are involved in implementing the vision?

- How many stakeholders could restate our vision in a clear, concise statement?

- How are our school goals aligned with our vision?

- How often is our vision referred to by school leaders, teachers and staff, students and parents, indicating that it is a compelling statement which inspires our community?

Improvement Strategies
Given our assessment of how well our school's vision statement is working, what more can we do to ensure that its power to align the school community behind a clear direction is continuously strengthened?

PROCEDURE: PART TWO (ALTERNATIVE IN-DEPTH EXERCISE)

1. You will be working with the other members of your team to create a triptych: a three-panel mural illustrating the work in which your school is engaged. The focus of each panel is as follows:
   - Panel 1: *WHAT*   What does our success look like? When we are successful in fulfilling our purpose, accomplishing our mission, and living up to our highest values, what does that look like? What contribution will our leadership team make to student achievement?
   - Panel 2: *HOW*   How is our success measured? How do we know we are achieving our goals? What observable evidence exists? How will our success translate into measurable results for student achievement?
   - Panel 3: *WHY*   Why is our success important? Why does it matter whether we are successful or not? To whom does it matter? What's at stake? What is our vision of the ultimate outcome of our success? What will it matter to student achievement?
2. Before beginning, discuss who are the target audiences for the messages you will be communicating through this mural (for example, students, parents, teachers and staff, the community, the school board, etc.) and what this means in terms of how the mural should be approached.
3. As a group, brainstorm what you think should be included in each panel. What are the main points you want to convey? What would be the most visually compelling ways of communicating these ideas?
4. Come to consensus as to which of the brainstormed ideas should be pictured in the mural.
5. Consider types of images, size of images, colors, placement, etc.
6. Decide who will draw which images, and then get to work.
7. When you are done, discuss how well the finished product accomplishes what you intended. Make any final refinements based on this assessment.
8. Prepare how you will present your mural to the rest of the school community.

3. Planning School Success

*It takes as much energy to wish
as it does to plan.*

—Eleanor Roosevelt

PURPOSE

While a compelling mission/vision statement is essential to your school's success, it is not sufficient. Without a plan for how that vision will be realized, people are likely to become disappointed, disillusioned, and demoralized. As George Carlin said, "Inside every cynical person, there is a disappointed idealist." I do believe that most educators are motivated by a desire to make a difference, and that leaders have an imperative to enable them to do so by creating an organization that supports their success.

The purpose of this lesson is to make sure that your school's goals are aligned with your vision and geared toward continuously improving students' learning. Part One continues the team assessment of leadership interactions using the *Leadership Outcomes Worksheet*. Part Two adds a new tool to your team's repertoire—Root Cause Analysis, which is designed to help uncover underlying causes of ineffective attempts to improve.

PROCEDURE: PART ONE

1. If you haven't already done so, decide who should be involved in the leadership interactions for this leadership outcome.
2. Refer to the model of the five foundations for successfully leading organizational change, and reflect on the implications for achieving continuous improvement at the school.
3. Communicate the leadership outcome for the second foundation related to using the *Leadership Outcomes Leadership Interactions (Team-Assessment) Goals/Strategies/Action Plans Worksheet*.
4. Now the team can conduct an assessment of the current situation using the suggested criteria from the worksheet as a guide.
5. Finally, the team can design Improvement Strategies for ensuring that this leadership outcome is strengthened and sustained.

Leadership Outcomes Leadership Interactions (Team-Assessment)
Goals/Strategies/Action Plans Worksheet

Leadership Outcome
All stakeholders share and support a set of strategic goals and action plans aimed at increasing student achievement, which they helped develop and are involved in implementing.

Current Assessment (Suggested Criteria)

• How specific and well defined are the goals?

• How directly are the goals linked to student achievement?

• Were the goals set on the basis of accurate data?

• How well are we using data to measure success in achieving the goals?

• How realistic are the goals?

• Are the action plans spelled out in terms of who, what, and when?

• Which of the school's goals is proving to be the most challenging for us to meet?

Improvement Strategies
Given our assessment of how well our school's strategic goals and action plans are working, what more can we do to ensure that its power to align the school community behind a clear direction is continuously strengthened?

PROCEDURE: PART TWO (ALTERNATIVE IN-DEPTH EXERCISE)

5 WHYS (Root Cause Analysis)

The 5 Whys strategy involves looking at any problem and asking: "Why?" and "What caused this problem?" By asking the question "Why" you can separate the symptoms from the causes of a problem, which is critical because if your solution only addresses a symptom and not the core issue, the problem will recur. 5 Whys has the advantage of being engaging, inexpensive, and easy to use.

1. Locate the goal that the team identified as proving to be the most challenging to meet on the *Leadership Outcomes Leadership Interactions (Team-Assessment) Goals/Strategies/Action Plans Worksheet.* Write this goal on a flip chart or white board.
2. Discuss what the problems are with achieving this goal until you've come to a shared understanding on what problem needs to be addressed.
3. Read the problem and ask other team members, "Why did this problem occur?" "What caused it?" Write the answer underneath the problem description.
4. Read the cause of the problem that was identified, and ask, "Why?" "What caused this to happen?"
5. Repeat this process three more times or until you arrive at what appears to be the root cause. (It may take more or less than 5 "whys," depending on the nature of the problem.)
6. It is important to validate that the proposed root causes are based on direct observation rather than on guesswork. So, before settling on a final root cause, ask the team members why they think it is correct. Here are some validating questions:
   • What research, evidence, or proof is there to support this root cause determination?
   • How confident are we that we have correctly identified the root cause? On what do we base our confidence?
   • Is there anything "underneath" the possible root cause that could be a more probable cause?

4. Allocating Resources to Support School Success

If you think education is expensive, try ignorance.

—DEREK BOK

PROCEDURE

With a Vision Statement and Goals/Action Plan in place, false starts toward change will occur unless the resources that are needed are available. Studies have found that schools that had linked resource use to their instructional improvement strategies achieved high levels of student performance. Some of the strategies used by these successful schools in aligning resources to student achievement include:

- Successful schools invest heavily in teacher training, which includes intensive 1- to 2-week summer institutes, longer teacher work years, resources for trainers, and, most important, placing instructional coaches in each school.
- Successful schools use state, local, and federal Title I funds to provide extra help for struggling students, which includes tutoring, extended-day academic help programs, summer school, and English language development for all ELL students.
- Successful schools use time more productively, which includes allocating more time for core subjects, offering double class periods at the secondary level in subjects where students are struggling to achieve the standards, and protecting classes from interruptions during core class periods.
- Successful schools create "professional learning communities," which includes teachers collaborating on the instructional program and in formative assessments analyses.

The purpose of this lesson is to determine how well your school allocates resources in order to provide maximum results for students. The procedure has two parts: a short assessment form and a more extensive evaluation.

PROCEDURE: PART ONE

1. If you haven't already done so, decide who should be involved in the leadership interactions for this third outcome. Since the team will be dealing with school finances, you might want to invite the district's business manager to participate.

2. Refer to the model of the five foundations for successfully leading organizational change, and reflect on the implications for achieving continuous improvement at the school.
3. Communicate the leadership outcome for the third foundation using the *Leadership Outcomes Leadership Interactions (Team-Assessment) Resources Worksheet.*
4. Now the team can conduct an assessment of the current situation using the suggested criteria from the worksheet as a guide.
5. Finally, the team can design Improvement Strategies for ensuring that this leadership outcome is strengthened and sustained.

Leadership Outcomes Leadership Interactions (Team-Assessment) Resources Worksheet

---

Leadership Outcome
Sufficient resources are available and allocated in alignment with the school's commitment to student achievement.

Current Assessment (Suggested Criteria)

- How obvious is the link between resource allocation and student achievement?

- To what extent was the resource allocation process based on a data-driven needs assessment?

- To what extent is stakeholder support sufficient to ensure success?

- To what extent are the financial resources sufficient to ensure success?

- To what extent are staff resources sufficient to ensure success?

- To what extent is the time dedicated to working on school improvement goals sufficient to ensure success?

Improvement Strategies
Given our assessment of how effectively our school's resources are allocated, what more can we do to ensure that they are being used to maximize our success with students?

PROCEDURE: PART TWO (ALTERNATIVE IN-DEPTH EXERCISE)

Visiting Team Analysis

1. Imagine you are an outside team of observers made up of a range of participants (teachers, administrators, parents, business and university partners, etc.) brought in to conduct an in-depth review of how well your school is performing in the area of aligning resources with instructional focus.[1]

2. Use the *In-Depth Review Summary Report Worksheet* to assess the school's level of accomplishment in the following four areas:
   - Integration of Funds—Funds, regardless of source, are combined to meet both the school's student performance goals and the needs of the professional learning community.
   - Uses of Teaching Personnel—The degree to which specialists, resource teachers, specially trained teachers, etc. are effectively used to meet the school's student performance goals.
   - Alignment—The degree to which the budget supports the school's instructional focus.
   - Time and Support—The degree to which the structure and schedule of the school day support the school's instructional objectives and learning goals.

3. As a result of your findings, identify three improvement strategies the school should employ to ensure that resources are being allocated to maximum benefit.

In-Depth Review Summary Report Worksheet

Assess the school's level of accomplishment in the following four areas.

Integration of Funds

How effectively are funds, regardless of source, integrated to meet both the school's student performance goals and the needs of the professional learning community?

Questions to consider:

1. What are the different funding sources? How are they managed? Are resources being combined to address the school's goals?

2. How are Title I and other external funds used within the school?

Uses of Teaching Personnel

How effectively are specialists, resource teachers, specially trained teachers, etc. used to meet the school's student performance goals?

In-Depth Review Summary Report Worksheet, *continued*

Questions to consider:

1. How did the school determine the learning needs of its students?

2. Are there any groups of students for whom learning needs have not been identified or no support services are being provided?

3. What evidence is there that the teams and individual teachers have sufficient access to additional expertise when needed?

Alignment

How effectively does the budget support the school's instructional focus?

Questions to consider:

1. How successful has the school been in attracting outside funding for focused instructional expansion?

2. How were decisions made regarding the budget and who was involved?

3. What evidence is there that the allocated portions of the budget support the school's instructional focus?

Time and Support

How effectively does the structure and schedule of the school day support the school's instructional objectives and learning goals?

Questions to consider:

1. What evidence is there that the allocation of time is designed to maximize instructional time and academic engagement time?

(*continues*)

In-Depth Review Summary Report Worksheet, *continued*

2. Are interruptions during key instructional activities kept to a minimum?

3. What evidence is there that the schedule is flexible enough to accommodate the need for more time in core academic subjects for some students?

4. What evidence is there that sufficient time is allocated and utilized for team meetings?

Improvement Strategies

As a result of your team's findings, what three improvement strategies do you recommend the school employ to ensure that resources are being allocated to maximum benefit?

1.

2.

3.

5. Developing Capacity for School Success

The best teachers teach the way kids learn.

—Pedro Noguera

PURPOSE

Now with your school's vision formulated, your goals and action plans articulated, and your resources allocated, expectations are high and so is the anxiety level. The next step to leading change successfully is to provide professional development training and coaching for the school's teachers and staff.

Assuming your school already has a professional development program, the purpose of this lesson is to evaluate its effectiveness and identify improvement strategies to ensure that investment in professional development activities yields maximum results in terms of student outcomes.

PROCEDURE: PART ONE

1. If you haven't already done so, decide who should be involved in the leadership interactions for this outcome. Consider if there are district resources with expertise in the design and evaluation of professional development programs who should be involved.
2. Refer to the Leadership for Change model of the five foundations (Table 5.1 on page 128) for successfully leading organizational change, and reflect on its implications for achieving continuous improvement at the school.
3. Communicate the leadership outcome for the fourth foundation using the *Leadership Outcomes Leadership Interactions (Team-Assessment) Training Worksheet.*
4. Now the team can conduct an assessment of the current situation using the suggested criteria from the worksheet as a guide.
5. Finally, the team can design Improvement Strategies for ensuring that this leadership outcome is strengthened and sustained.

Leadership Outcomes Leadership Interactions (Team-Assessment) Training Worksheet

Leadership Outcome

All staff members are participating in a professional development program focused on effective teaching and learning, which they helped design and evaluate.

Current Assessment (Suggested Criteria)

- What are the student learning outcomes that the professional development program is designed to achieve? What student assessments were used to identify these goals?

- What has been the impact of the professional development program on student learning? How is this being evaluated?

- What instructional practices have proven to be effective in producing these student Learning Outcomes?

- What knowledge and skills do teachers and other relevant staff need to have in order to successfully implement these instructional practices?

- What types of experiences (e.g., collaborative planning, organized study groups, workshops, online learning, structured opportunities for practice with feedback, etc.) enable teachers and staff to acquire the required knowledge and skills?

- What has been the impact of the professional development program on teacher practice? How is this being measured?

- What has been the teachers' response to the professional development program? How was this assessed?

- What recommendations have they made in terms of how professional development experiences can be planned, designed, and implemented to better meet their needs?

Leadership Outcomes Leadership Interactions (Team-Assessment) Training Worksheet, *continued*

Improvement Strategies

Given our assessment of how effectively our school's professional development program is addressing the needs of staff and enhancing student learning, what more can we do to ensure that they are being used to maximize our success with students?

PROCEDURE: PART TWO (ALTERNATIVE IN-DEPTH EXERCISE)

How School Leaders Learn How to Lead

1. Imagine you are on the school district's Professional Development Committee, and you've been asked to plan and implement a school leadership program. Use the *How School Leaders Learn How to Lead Professional Development Program Worksheet* to explore the areas that characterize an exemplary program for developing school leaders.

After you've completed the worksheet, address the following two questions as they apply to your school:

- Given your analysis of what would be the most effective school leadership development program, what's *missing* in your current program? What steps can you take to improve your program?
- Given your analysis of what would be the most effective school leadership development program, what *obstacles* are limiting the success of your current program? What steps can you take to overcome these obstacles?

How School Leaders Learn How to Lead Professional Development Program Worksheet

---

- What student learning outcomes are most subject to the influence of leadership actions of individual school leaders?

- What student learning outcomes are most subject to the influence of leadership inter-actions of school leadership teams?

(*continues*)

How School Leaders Learn How to Lead Professional Development Program Worksheet, *continued*

- How can school leaders have an impact directly on these student learning outcomes?

- How can school leaders have an impact indirectly on these student learning outcomes?

- What knowledge, attitudes, skills, and behaviors do school leaders need in order to have a significant impact on student learning outcomes?

- What types of learning experiences could be used to develop the necessary knowledge, attitudes, skills, and behaviors?

- What organizational support and resources would be needed for the successful implementation of this program?

- If you could design the most effective school leadership program, what would be included in the curriculum?

6. Measuring and Rewarding School Success

This vision of the future must be formulated in such a way that it will make the pain of changing worth the effort.

—Noel M. Tichy and Mary Anne Devanna

PURPOSE

After my first book was translated into Russian, I was invited to travel to Russia as part of an international youth leadership program. Conducting workshops in various communities across the country sounded like an amazing opportunity and a great adventure. When I was informed that I needed to commit to being there for two weeks, I was concerned about being away from home and from my other clients for such an extended period of time. The fact that I was only going to be paid the equivalent of two days of consulting time for two weeks of work didn't help.

Then I discovered that we would be traveling across Russia by train, and would be staying in army barracks throughout the trip. I must say my enthusiasm was beginning to wane. The scales finally tipped in the direction of taking a pass, when I was told that due to political unrest in the country, the sponsors of the program could not guarantee my security. I might have been willing to give up some of my time, money, and creature comforts, but I had to draw the line on my life. I'm afraid the risks outweighed the rewards.

Forget all you know about human motivation. It pretty much boils down to a cost/benefit analysis. When faced with the choice of taking a particular action or not, we will—consciously or unconsciously—calculate the potential upside, the benefits of doing it, versus the downside, the cost of doing it. If the benefits outweigh the costs, we'll do it. If the costs are too great, we won't. It should be noted that costs and benefits are in the eyes of the beholder. What is perceived as a benefit to one person may be perceived by someone else as a cost. An outgoing student, for example, might relish the chance to speak in front of the class, while a shy student would be mortified by the prospect of having to do so.

This is relevant to managing change within an organization because if the people who are being asked to do something differently do not see the benefit in it, then they will resist. You may have an inspiring vision and a smart set of goals and action plans, resources may be aligned and training may be happening; yet if there are no real incentives, the results will be spotty at best. Some individuals might be motivated, but significant and sustained change requires an intelligent, organizational approach to ensure that the majority of people are rewarded for their efforts.

The purpose of this lesson is to assess your school's capacity for and/or resistance to change. While there may be an expressed desire for more distributed leadership, for example, the cost of giving up control and decision-making autonomy at the top of the organization may be a price some administrators are not willing to pay. Teachers may recognize the value of greater collaboration with their peers to improve teaching practices, but if it means reworking years' worth of lesson plans, then maybe, for some, sticking with the old tried and true methods is better.

PROCEDURE: PART ONE

1. If you haven't already done so, decide who should be involved in the leadership interaction for each of these outcomes.
2. Refer to the Leadership for Change model of the five foundations (Table 5.1 on page 128) for successfully leading organizational change, and reflect on its implications for achieving continuous improvement at the school.
3. Communicate the leadership outcome for the fifth foundation related to using the *Leadership Outcomes Leadership Interactions (Team-Assessment) Incentives Worksheet.*
4. Now the team can conduct an assessment of the current situation using the suggested criteria from the worksheet as a guide.
5. Next, the team can design Improvement Strategies for ensuring that this leadership outcome is strengthened and sustained.
6. Using the Improvement Strategies identified by the team, develop and administer a survey for teachers, parents, and students so as to validate the team's assessment, as well as to engage the rest of the school community in creating incentives for improving student performance.

Leadership Outcomes Leadership Interactions (Team-Assessment) Incentives Worksheet

Leadership Outcome

All members of the school community are genuinely motivated and experience a high level of satisfaction because they see their efforts paying off in ways that are measurable for students, and rewarding for them.

**Leadership Outcomes Leadership Interactions (Team-Assessment) Incentives
Worksheet,** *continued*

Current Assessment

From the context of the *school leaders:*

- What's being asked?

- What are the benefits?

- What are the costs?

- Is it worth it?

Improvement Strategies

What could be done to increase the benefits and reduce the costs so that the perceived value
is compellingly obvious?

Current Assessment

From the context of the *teachers:*

- What's being asked?

- What are the benefits?

- What are the costs?

- Is it worth it?

(*continues*)

Leadership Outcomes Leadership Interactions (Team-Assessment) Incentives Worksheet, *continued*

Improvement Strategies

What could be done to increase the benefits and reduce the costs so that the perceived value is compellingly obvious?

Current Assessment

From the context of the *parents:*

- What's being asked?

- What are the benefits?

- What are the costs?

- Is it worth it?

Improvement Strategies

What could be done to increase the benefits and reduce the costs so that the perceived value is compellingly obvious?

Current Assessment

From the context of the *students:*

- What's being asked?

- What are the benefits?

Leadership Outcomes Leadership Interactions (Team-Assessment) Incentives Worksheet, *continued*

- What are the costs?

- Is it worth it?

Improvement Strategies

What could be done to increase the benefits and reduce the costs so that the perceived value is compellingly obvious?

In Conclusion

The main point to remember from this part of the book is that schools—like any organization—require a coordinated effort to create and sustain meaningful change.

- Resistance to change occurs under the following circumstances:
  - People don't recognize that there is a problem.
  - People recognize there is a problem, but they don't believe there is a solution.
  - People recognize there is a problem, they believe there is a solution, but they don't think the solution being proposed is the right one.
  - People recognize there is a problem, they believe the right solution has been proposed, but they don't trust that you are capable of effectively leading them to solve it.
- This brings us back to clarity, concern, and competence being the critical characteristics of effective leadership.
- Everything you need to know about human motivation can be summed up as a cost/benefit analysis. If the benefits as you perceive them are worth the cost, you will be motivated to act. So, the bottom line is: What's in it for you to act on the lessons you learned by reading this book?

SUMMARY

*Humans are ambitious and rational and proud. And we don't fall
in line with people who don't respect us and who don't have our
best interests at heart. We are willing to follow leaders, but only to
the extent that we believe they call on our best, not on our worst.*

—RACHEL MADDOW

My goal in writing this book was to support your success by providing you with a practical guide based on current research about what's working in schools, as well as my 30 years of experience facilitating leadership development workshops for educators, business executives, and leaders of nonprofit organizations. Some readers might quibble with my choice of topics. Others may find fault with my emphasis on "soft skills" over other critical areas such as data analysis. Fair enough.

On the other hand, when I think about people in my life who called on the best in me, who I felt respected me and had my best interests at heart, I remember individuals who connected with me in a meaningful way. As when I showed up late for the first day of kindergarten. The teacher had already started class. All the other pupils were present. Musical instruments had been distributed to each child. There were none left by the time I arrived. I was scared, and prepared to be left out. To my surprise, the teacher welcomed me warmly, handed me a pencil to use as a baton, and invited me to serve as the orchestra leader. I still remember that act of kindness.

So yes, I got good grades in school, and that was important. I learned valuable concepts and developed my cognitive skills, and these have stood me well. But the teachers who made the biggest difference, and the moments I most vividly remember, all had an affective component. My character has been shaped by the touch of human connection, compassion, and caring.

While I would hope that everything contained in this book is of value to you, I am highlighting the following summary points. Each of the five parts of the book should lead to a core commitment on your part since, without commitment, there is unlikely to be the determination needed to succeed.

THE 5 COMMITMENTS OF EFFECTIVE SCHOOL LEADERS

1. *Commit to being responsible.* Your choosing to read a book on school leadership suggests that greatness, not mediocrity, is your mission. As Winston Churchill said, "The price of greatness is responsibility." Don't just accept responsibility but embrace it, and challenge others to do the same. I know of no other way to achieve greatness.

2. *Commit to acting with integrity.* You cannot lead if you are not trusted. For others to trust you, they need to know they can count on you. Deliver on your promises. Keep your agreements. Demonstrate that your word is good. Hold others accountable for doing what they said they would. I know of no better way to reduce the drama and dysfunction in organizations, and to create a safe and sane learning environment.

3. *Commit to doing what it takes to achieve your goals.* Being a school leader is difficult. So is being a teacher. So is being a student. There are many good reasons why goals set don't get met. Obstacles abound. Remember, you can have what you want in life, or you can have the excuses why you don't. If adults can't overcome adversity to achieve the success they envision, what hope do students have?

4. *Commit to inspiring and instituting improvement in teaching and learning.* Every teacher is in a position to have a positive impact on the life and learning of many students. Whether he or she has the capacity to do so is—to a great extent—up to you. How much of your day is spent monitoring the quality of teaching and learning? What else are you doing instead that is of greater importance?

5. *Commit to balancing your idealism with a daily dose of reality.* The French writer René Daumal wrote: "Keep your eye fixed on the path to the top, but don't forget to look right in front of you. The last step depends on the first. Don't think you're there just because you see the summit. Watch your footing, be sure of the next step, but don't let that distract you from the highest goal. The first step depends on the last." Being an effective leader requires both a vision of a better future, as well as a plan for achieving it.

If you want to know how great a leader you are, turn around and see who's following. If you are not impressed, then honor the above commitments, and check again in a few months.

My commitment to you is to respond if you reach out, and to help you grow as an effective school leader in whatever ways I can. I would appreciate knowing the extent to which you were able to use the tips, tools, and templates in this book at your school or district. You can reach me at FrankSiccone.com. Thanks and best wishes.

ENDNOTES

Preface

1. Miller, Ashley. (2009, October 5). *Principal turnover: Student achievement and teacher retention.* Princeton University. Retrieved from http://www.ers.princeton.edu/Miller.pdf

2. The Interstate School Leaders Licensure Consortium (ISLLC) Standards were developed by the Council of Chief State School Officers (CCSSO) and member states. Copies may be downloaded from the Council's Web site: http://www.ccsso.org

Part One: To Lead Is to Learn—Confidence Skills

1. National Staff Development Council. (2000, December 1). *Learning to lead, leading to learn: Improving school quality through principal professional development.* Retrieved from http://www.nsdc.org/library/leaders/leader_report.cfm

2. Hirsch, Eric, & Emerick, Scott (with Church, Keri, & Fuller, Ed). (2007). *Teacher working conditions are student learning conditions.* Chapel Hill, NC: Center for Teacher Quality. Report on the 2006 North Carolina Teacher Working Conditions Survey. Retrieved from http://www.teachingquality.org/pdfs/twcnc2006.pdf

3. Sources that provide information on the background and use of the PDSA Cycle include: Deming, W. Edwards. (1982). *Out of the crisis.* Cambridge, MA: MIT Press.

   Rinehart, Gary. (1993). *Quality education: Using the philosophy of Dr. W. Edwards Deming to transform the educational system.* Milwaukee, WI: ASQ Quality Press.

   Guide to using data in school improvement efforts. (2004). Naperville, IL: Learning Point Associates.

4. Baldrige.com. (2009, October 2). *Education: PDSA + quality tools + AYP.* Retrieved from http://www.baldrige.com/sector/education/education-pdsa-quality-tools-ayp/

5. Gosmire, Doreen, Morrison, Marcia, & Van Osdel, Joanne. (2009, June 8). Administrators' and teacher's perceptions of the value and current use of the ELCC Standards. *NCPEA Educational Leadership Review (ELR), 10*(2). Retrieved from http://cnx.org/content/m24426/1.2/

6. Some of the case studies in this section were adapted from Remley, Theodore P. Jr., & Huey, Wayne C. (2002, October). An ethics quiz for school counselors. Special issue: Legal and ethical issues in school counseling. *Professional School Counseling, 6*(1), 1–11.

Part Two: To Lead Is to Listen—Communication Skills

1. "Have a Heart" activity adapted with permission from *Training high school conflict managers,* p. SF-9 (revised 1996) by Community Board Program, San Francisco. All rights reserved. Visit http://www.communityboards.org for more information.

2. Communication styles are based on the work of William Moulton Marston originally published in 1928, and then further developed with Walter V. Clarke in 1948.

Part Three: To Lead Is to Align—Collaboration Skills

1. Balancing inquiry and advocacy adapted with permission from Ross, Rick, & Roberts, Charlotte. (1994). In Peter M. Senge, et al., *The fifth discipline fieldbook: Strategies and tools for building a learning organization* (pp. 253–259). New York: Crown Business.

2. Gerzon, Mark. (2006). *Leading through conflict: How successful leaders transform differences into opportunities* (p. 106). Cambridge, MA: Harvard Business Press.

3. Losada, Marcial, & Heaphy, Emily. (2004). The role of positivity and connectivity in performance of business teams: A nonlinear dynamic model. *American Behavioral Scientist, 47*(6), 740–765.

4. Decision-making styles adapted with permission from *Mastering meetings for results.* (1986). San Francisco: Interaction Associates.

5. Suggestions included in this activity are attributed to Maryland Coalition for Inclusive Education. (2008). *Finding collaborative planning time.* Retrieved from http://www.mcieinclusiveschools.org

6. Cardno, Carol. (1998). *Making a difference by managing dilemmas.* Research information for teachers, Set 1. Retrieved from http://www.educationalleaders.govt.nz/Media/Files/Making-a-difference-by-managing dilemmas

Part Four: To Lead Is to Teach—Coaching Skills

1. Turnbull, Brenda J., Haslam, M. Bruce, Arcaira, Erikson R., Riley, Derek L., Sinclair, Beth, & Coleman, Stephen. (2009, December). How principals manage their time is key to improving instruction in their schools. In *Evaluation of the school administration manager project.* Educational Research Newsletter. Policy Studies Associates, Inc. for the Wallace Foundation. Retrieved from http://www.ernweb.com/public/1175cfm

2. Robinson, Viviane. (2007, April). How school leaders make a difference to their students. Paper presented at the International Confederation of Principals, Auckland.

3. National Association of Elementary School Principles. (2008, September/October). Standards for leading learning communities: A call to action. *Principal.* Retrieved from http://www.naesp.org.

4. Veenman, Simon, & Denessen, Eddie. (2001). The coaching of teachers: Results of five training studies. *Educational Research and Evaluation, 7*(4), 385–417.

5. Ferriter, Bill. (2010, Dec. 17). The tempered radical, teacher leaders. *Network.* Retrieved from http://teacherleaders.typepad.com/the_tempered_radical/2010/10/classroom-walkthroughs-and-checklist-leadership.html/

6. Bloom, Gary, Castagna, Claire, & Warren, Betsy. (2006, May). More than mentors: Principal coaching. May/June 2003 edition of Leadership Association of California School Administrators. *Educational Leadership, 32*(5), 20–23.

Part Five: To Lead Is to Succeed—Continuous Improvement Skills

1. Activity suggested by *In-depth review: Boston Public Schools school accountability system, 2000–2001.* Retrieved from http://www.boston.k12.ma.us/agassiz/awidrresources.html

BIBLIOGRAPHY

Alessandra, Tony, & O'Connor, Michael. (1994). *People smarts: Bending the golden rule to give others what they want.* San Diego, CA: Pfeiffer & Company.

Allison, Elle. (2008, Winter). Coaching teachers for school transformation. *Principal Matters, 75,* 9–10. Retrieved from http://www.wisdomout.com/PDF/CoachingTeachersforSchool Transformation.pdf

Baldoni, John. (2009, Sept. 30). How to develop your leadership pitch. *Harvard Business Review.* Retrieved from http://blogs.hbr.org/baldoni/2009/09/how_to_develop_your_leadership.html.

Baldrige.com. (2009, Oct. 2). *Education: PDSA + quality tools + AYP.* Retrieved from http://www.baldrige.com/sector/education/education-pdsa-quality-tools-ayp/.

Bennis, Warren, & Goldsmith, Joan. (2010). *Learning to lead.* New York: Basic Books.

Bloom, Gary, Castagna, Claire, Moir, Ellen, & Warren, Betsy. (2005). *Blended coaching: Skills and strategies to support principal development.* Thousand Oaks, CA: Corwin.

Burns, James MacGregor. (1978). *Leadership.* New York: Harper & Row.

Cardno, Carol. (1998). *Making a difference by managing dilemmas.* Research information for teachers, Set 1. Retrieved from http://www.educationalleaders.govt.nz/Media/Files/Making-a-difference-by-managing-dilemmas

Cardno, Carol. (2007). Leadership learning—the praxis of dilemma management. *International Studies in Educational Administration, 35*(2), 33–50.

Cheliotes, Linda Gross, & Reilly, Marceta Fleming. (2010). *Coaching conversations: Transforming your school one conversation at a time.* Thousand Oaks, CA: Corwin.

Clifford, Matthew. (2010, February). *Hiring quality school leaders: Challenges and emerging practices.* Naperville, IL: Learning Point Associates. Retrieved from http://www.learningpt.org.

Cohen, Dan S. (2005). *The heart of change field guide.* Boston: Harvard Business School Press.

Collins, Jim. (2001). *Good to great: Why some companies make the leap . . . and others don't.* New York: HarperCollins.

Cosner, Shelby, & Peterson, Kent. (2003, May–June). Building a learning community: Instructional leadership is a thoughtful journey that builds and sustains learning cultures as well as learning structures. *Leadership, 32*(5), 12–15.

Council of Chief State School Officers. (2008). *Interstate School Leaders Licensure Consortium (ISLLC) Standards for School Leaders.* Washington, DC: Author.

Covey, Stephen R. (1989). *The seven habits of highly effective people.* New York: Simon and Schuster.

Davis, Stephen, Darling-Hammond, Linda, LaPointe, Michelle, & Meyerson, Debra. (2005). *School leadership study: Developing successful principals* (Review of Research). Stanford, CA: Stanford University, Stanford Educational Leadership Institute.

Deming, Edwards W. (1982). *Out of the crisis.* Cambridge, MA: MIT Press.

Donohoo, Jenni, & Hannay, Lynne. (2009, January). Sustaining school improvement through collaborative action research. Paper presented at the 22nd International Congress for School Effectiveness and Improvement. Vancouver, BC, Canada.

Downey, Carolyn J., Steffy, Betty E., Poston, William K., & English, Fenwick W. (2009). *Advancing the three-minute walk-through: Mastering reflective practice.* Thousand Oaks, CA: Corwin.

DuFour, Richard. (2004, May). What is a professional learning community? *Educational Leadership, 61*(8), 6–11. ASCD.

DuFour, Richard, DuFour, Rebecca, Eaker, Robert, & Karhanek, Gayle. (2004). *Whatever it takes: How a professional learning community responds when kids don't learn.* Bloomington, IN: Solution Tree.

Elmore, Richard F. (2004). *School reform from the inside out: Policy, practice, and performance.* Boston: Harvard Education Press.

Farber, Steve. (2004). *Radical leap: A personal lesson in extreme leadership.* Chicago: Dearborn Trade Publishing.

Fleming, David. (2001). Narrative leadership: Using the power of stories. *Strategy & Leadership, 29*(4), 34–36.

Fleming, Grace L., & Leo, Tara. (1999). Principals and teachers: Continuous learners. Issues . . . about change. *Southwest Educational Development Laboratory, 7*(2). Retrieved from http://www.sedl.org/change/issues/issues72/

Fournies, Ferdinand F. (1978). *Coaching for improved work performance.* Blue Ridge Summit, PA: Liberty Hall Press.

Francis, Dave, & Young, Don. (1979). *Improving work groups: A practical manual for team building.* San Diego, CA: University Associates.

Gamage, David, Adams, Don, & McCormack, Ann. (2009, January–March). How does a school leader's role influence student achievements? A review of research findings and best practices. *International Journal of Educational Leadership Preparation, 4*(1). Retrieved from http://cnx.org/content/m19751/latest/

Garfield, Charles. (1992). *Second to none: How our smartest companies put people first.* Homewood, IL: Business One Irwin.

Gerzon, Mark. (2006). *Leading through conflict: How successful leaders transform differences into opportunities.* Cambridge, MA: Harvard Business Press.

Gosmire, Doreen, Morrison, Marcia, & Van Osdel, Joanne. (2009, June 8). Administrators' and teachers' perceptions of the value and current use of the ELCC standards. *Connexions.* Retrieved from http://cnx.org/content/m24426/1.2/

Guide to using data in school improvement efforts. (2004). Naperville, IL: Learning Point Associates.

Guskey, Thomas R. (2000). *Evaluating professional development.* Thousand Oaks, CA: Corwin.

Hallinger, Philip. (2008, March). Methodologies for studying school leadership: A review of 25 years of research using the principal instructional management rating scale. Paper presented at the Annual Meeting of the American Educational Research Association, New York.

Halverson, Richard, Grigg, Jeffrey, Prichett, Reid, & Thomas, Chris. (2005, July). The new instructional leadership: Creating data-driven instructional systems in schools. School of Education, Department of Educational Leadership and Policy Analysis, University of Wisconsin-Madison. Paper presented at Annual Meeting of the National Council of Professors of Educational Administration, Washington, DC.

Harris, Alma. (2005, May). Leading or misleading? Distributed leadership and school improvement. *Journal of Curriculum Studies, 37*(3), 255–265. Retrieved from http://faculty.ed.uiuc.edu/westbury/jcs/

Higgins, James M. (2005). *101 Creative problem solving techniques: The handbook of new ideas for business.* Winter Park, FL: New Management Publishing.

Hirsch, Eric, & Emerick, Scott (with Church, Keri & Fuller, Ed.). (2007). *Teacher working conditions are student learning conditions*. Chapel Hill, NC: Center for Teacher Quality. Report on the 2006 North Carolina Teacher Working Conditions Survey. Retrieved from http://www.teachingquality.org/pdfs/twcnc2006.pdf

Jenkins, Billy. (2009, January–February). What it takes to be an instructional leader. *Principal, 88*(3), 34–37.

Jerald, Craig. (2008). *Helping schools engage in collaborative, strategic problem solving.* Center for Comprehensive School Reform and Improvement. Naperville, IL: Learning Point Associates. Retrieved from http://www.learningpt.org

Killion, Joellen. (2002). *Assessing impact: Evaluating staff development.* Oxford, OH: National Staff Development Council.

Kouzes, James M., & Posner, Barry Z. (2002). *The leadership challenge: How to get extraordinary things done in organizations.* San Francisco: Jossey-Bass.

Lambert, Linda. (2005, Spring). What does leadership capacity really mean? *Journal of Staff Development, 26*(2). Retrieved from http://www.nsdc.org/members/jsd/lambert262.pdf

Langley, Gerald J., Moen, Ronald, Nolan, Kevin M., Nolan, Thomas W., Norman, Clifford L., & Provost, Lloyd P. (2009). *The improvement guide: A practical approach to enhancing organizational performance.* San Francisco: Jossey-Bass.

Lashway, Larry. (2003, Summer). Distributed leadership. *Research Roundup, 19*(4), 1–4.

Leithwood, Kenneth, Louis, Karen Seashore, Anderson, Stephen, & Wahlstrom, Kyla. (2004). *How leadership influences student learning.* New York: Wallace Foundation.

Losada, Marcial, & Heaphy, Emily. (2004, February). The role of positivity and connectivity in performance of business teams: A nonlinear dynamic model. *American Behavioral Scientist, 47*(6), 740–765.

Marston, William Moulton. (1928). *Emotions of normal people.* New York: Harcourt, Brace & Co..

Merrill, M. David. (2001). Instructional strategies and learning styles: Which takes precedence? In Robert Reiser and Jack Dempsey (Eds.), *Trends and issues in instructional technology,* 99–106. Columbus, OH: Prentice Hall.

Miller, Ashley. (2009, October 5). *Principal turnover: Student achievement and teacher retention.* Princeton University. Retrieved from http://www.ers.princeton.edu/Miller.pdf.

National Association of Elementary School Principals. (2008, September–October). Standards for leading learning communities: A call to action. *Principal.* Retrieved from http://www.naesp.org.

National Association of Secondary Schools. (2010). *10 Skills for effective school leaders.* Reston, VA: NASSP.

National Staff Development Council. (2000, Dec. 1). Learning to lead, leading to learn: Improving school quality through principal professional development. Retrieved from http://www.nsdc.org/library/leaders/leader_report.cfm

Odden, Allan, & Archibald, Sarah. (2000). *Reallocating resources: How to boost student achievement without asking for more.* Thousand Oaks, CA: Corwin.

Odden, Allan, Pincus, Lawrence O., Archibald, Sarah, Goetz, Michael, Mangan, Michelle Turner, & Aportela, Anabel. (2007). *Moving from good to great in Wisconsin: Funding schools adequately and doubling student performance.* Madison: University of Wisconsin, Wisconsin Center for Education Research, Consortium for Policy Research in Education.

Organisation for Economic Co-operation and Development (OECD). (2008, August).

Improving school leadership. Vol. 1: *Policy and practice.* Retrieved from http://www.oecd.org/edu/schoolleadership

Organisation for Economic Co-operation and Development (OECD). (2009). *Improving school leadership. The toolkit.* Retrieved from http://www.oecd.org/edu/schoolleadership

Osborn, Alex F. (1993). *Applied imagination: Principles and procedures of creative problem solving* (3rd ed.). Amherst, MA: Creative Education Foundation.

Perkins, David. (2002). *King Arthur's round table: How collaborative conversations create smart organizations.* New York: Wiley.

Perkins, David. (2009a). *Making learning whole: How seven principles of teaching can transform education.* San Francisco: Jossey-Bass.

Perkins, David. (2009b). Developing leaders and leadership in organizations. *Usable Knowledge.* Harvard Business School of Education. Retrieved from http://www.uknow.gse.harvard.edu/leadership/leadership003b.html

Peters, Tom, & Austin, Nancy. (1985). *A passion for excellence.* New York: Random House.

Raymond, Margaret. (2008, April). *Paying for A's: An early exploration of student reward and incentive programs in charter schools.* Stanford, CA: Center for Research on Education Outcome (CREDO), Stanford University.

Reeves, Douglas. (2004). *Assessing educational leaders.* Thousand Oaks, CA: Corwin.

Remley, Theodore P. Jr., & Huey, Wayne C. (2002, October). An ethics quiz for school counselors. Special issue: Legal and ethical issues in school counseling. *Professional School Counseling, 6*(1), 1–11. American School Counselor Association.

Rinehart, Gary. (1993). *Quality education: Using the philosophy of Dr. W. Edwards Deming to transform the educational system.* Milwaukee, WI: ASQ Quality Press.

Robinson, Viviane. (2007, April). How school leaders make a difference to their students. Paper presented at the International Confederation of Principals, Auckland.

Senge, Peter M. (1990). *The fifth discipline: The art and practice of the learning organization.* New York: Doubleday/Currency.

Senge, Peter M., Kleiner, Art, Roberts, Charlotte, & Ross, Rick. (1994). *The fifth discipline fieldbook: Strategies and tools for building a learning organization.* New York: Crown Business.

Senge, Peter M., Cambron McCabe, Nelda H., Lucas, Timothy, Kleiner, Art, Dutton, Janis, & Smith, Bryan. (2000). *Schools that learn: A fifth discipline fieldbook for educators, parents, and everyone who cares about education.* New York: Crown Business.

Siccone, Frank. (1997). *The power to lead: A guidebook for school administrators on facilitating change.* Boston: Allyn & Bacon.

Siccone, Frank, & Canfield, Jack. (1993). *101 Ways to develop student self-esteem and responsibility.* Boston: Allyn & Bacon.

Siccone, Frank, & McCarty, Hanoch. (2001). *Motivating your students: Before you can teach them, you have to reach them.* Boston: Allyn & Bacon.

Silberman, Charles E. (1970). *Crisis in the classroom: The remaking of American education.* New York: Random House.

Sparks, Dennis. (2002, October). *Taking personal responsibility for professional development that improves student learning.* California Staff Development Council. Retrieved from http://www.learningforward.org/news/authors/SparksBrief.pdf

Spillane, James P., & Diamond, John B. (2007). *Distributed leadership in practice.* New York: Teachers College Press.

Steiner, Lucy, & Kowal, Julie. (2007). *Principal as instructional leader: Designing a coaching program that fits.* Center for Comprehensive School Reform and Improvement. Naperville, IL: Learning

Point Associates. Retrieved from http://www.learningpt.org

Straker, David. (1997). *Rapid problem solving with post-it notes.* Cambridge, MA: DaCapo Press.

Straw, Julie. (2002). *The 4-dimensional manager: DiSC strategies for managing different people in the best ways.* San Francisco: Berrett-Koehler.

Tieger, Paul D., & Barron-Tieger, Barbara. (1998). *The art of speed-reading people: Harness the power of personality type and create what you want in business and in life.* Boston: Little, Brown and Company.

Turnbull, Brenda J., Haslam, M. Bruce, Arcaira, Erikson R., Riley, Derek L., Sinclair, Beth, & Coleman, Stephen. (2009, December). How principals manage their time is key to improving instruction in their schools. In *Evaluation of the school administration manager project.* Educational Research Newsletter. Policy Studies Associates, Inc. for the Wallace Foundation. Retrieved from http://www.ernweb.com/public/1175cfm

Von Oech, Roger. (1986). *A kick in the seat of the pants.* New York: Harper & Row.

Vescio, Vicki, Ross, Dorene, & Adams, Alyson. (2006, Jan.). A review of research on professional learning communities: What do we know? Paper presented at the NSRF Research Forum, University of Florida.

Walton, Donald. (1989). *Are you communicating? You can't manage without it.* New York: McGraw-Hill.

West-Burnham, John. (2004). Building leadership capacity—helping leaders learn. NCSL thinkpiece. National College for School Leadership, United Kingdom. *Educational Leaders.* Retrieved from http://forms.ncsl.org.uk/mediastore/image2/randd-building-lead-capacity.pdf

Wood, Julia T. (2009). *Interpersonal communication: Everyday encounters.* Belmont, CA: Wadsworth Publishing.

Zepeda, Sally J. (2009). *The instructional leader's guide to informal classroom observations.* Larchmont, NY: Eye on Education.

INDEX